MW00617680

I Can't Hear God Anymore

Life in a Dallas Cult

All interviews were conducted in confidentiality and the real names of interviewees are withheld by mutual agreement.

Published by VM Life Resources, LLC
PO Box 126
Rowlett, Texas 75030-0126
www.vmliferesources.com

ISBN: 0-977660-0-X

Library of Congress Catalog Card Number: 2006920420
Printed in the United States of America

10 9 8 7 6 5 4 3 2 1

Cover design by Bruce De Roos, Graphic Designer
Book Design & Typesetting by SunEditWrite.com

Except where indicated, the Bible quotations contained herein are from the King James Bible.

Revised Standard Version Bible (RSV), copyright 1946, 1952 by the Division of Christian Education of the National Council of the Churches of Christ in the United States of America. Used by permission. All rights reserved.

Grateful acknowledgment is made to the following for permission to reprint or adapt previously published material:

Augsburg Fortress Publishers: Excerpt from *The New Testament and the People of God* by N.T. Wright. Copyright © 1992 by Nicholas Thomas Wright. Reprinted by permission of Augsburg Fortress Publishers.

The Dallas Morning News: Excerpt from "Chance Encounter Has Chain Reaction," published on August 17, 1968. Reprinted by permission from *The Dallas Morning News*. One-time, nonexclusive, non-transferable copyright permission to reprint the quotation is granted provided that excerpting the quotation from the article does not change its essential meaning. Requirements include no suggestion of an endorsement by this newspaper for any particular product or service and no use of *The Dallas Morning News*' flag. Other than the rights specified herein, no other rights have been granted, and further permission is required for other uses. No archiving of the content is permitted.

North Atlantic Books/Frog, Ltd: Excerpt from *The Guru Papers: Marks of Authoritarian Power* by Joel Kramer & Diana Alstad. Copyright © 1993 by Joel Kramer & Diana Alstad. Reprinted by permission of North Atlantic Books/ Frog, Ltd.

Red Wheel/Weiser: Excerpt from *The Spear of Destiny* by Trevor Ravenscroft. Copyright © 1973 by Trevor Ravenscroft. Reprinted by permission of Red Wheel/Weiser.

University of North Carolina Press: Excerpt from *Thought Reform and the Psychology of Totalism: A Study of 'Brainwashing' in China* by Robert Jay Lifton. Copyright © 1989 by Robert Jay Lifton. Reprinted by permission of University of North Carolina Press.

Waterbrook Press: Adapted from *Toxic Faith*. Copyright© 1991, 2001 by Stephen Arterburn and Jack Felton. Reprinted by permission of WaterBrook Press, Colorado Springs, Colorado. All rights reserved.

W.W. Norton & Company: Excerpt from *Recovery From Cults: Help for Victims of Psychological and Spiritual Abuse* by Michael D. Langone, editor. Copyright © 1993 by American Family Foundation. Used by permission of W.W. Norton & Company, Inc.

In loving memory of
Crystal Humphress Daniel

Remember that none of us is beyond being manipulated by an intense, dedicated, and persistent persuader who meets us at a time when we are vulnerable, needy, and lonely.

Margaret Thaler Singer
Author, *Cults in Our Midst*

ACKNOWLEDGMENTS

So many people have made this book possible. My sister, Joan Hand, was the first person to tell me I should write a book about my experience at Trinity Foundation. I thought at the time that it was a preposterous suggestion, but she envisioned this book before I did and she encouraged me every step of the way. I am eternally grateful for my counselor, Debbie Devine. Doug and I may never have married or left Trinity Foundation without her skillful counseling. Debbie also suggested I write this book, but it was not until Crystal died and I found an old e-mail she sent me encouraging me to write a book — "one of enlightenment and not anger" — that I realized that this was something God was directing. I will always be grateful for Sherry Lewis, who is one of my dearest friends. Thank you for being there throughout the writing and for always being available to listen to me and pray for and with me. Also, I could not have written this book without the help of Rick Robertson, who provided many hours in helping me understand the early days of the Trinity Foundation. Because of his hard work in recovery from the negative aspects of Trinity Foundation, he was instrumental in my own recovery. I am also indebted to all the former members, both to those who provided hours of their time in interviews and to those who were unable to participate because it was too painful to remember their experience at Trinity Foundation. All of them were an inspiration to me and kept me going when I wanted to give up. I pray that this book does justice to their stories. Special thanks to the "party girls" (a name that is no way indicative of the nature of this group, but one that we are stuck with): the late Anita Battershell, Victoria Boyer, Sonya Gaines, Sandy King, Melody Kuhns, Arlene Shorter, and Ann Turbeville. You are precious friends and you make my life richer. Thank you for standing by me when I was a member of Trinity Foundation and during my transition out. Special thanks also to Gene Clark who provided untold hours reading and editing the manuscript. Gene was an enormous support and gave me invaluable feedback. I will be forever grateful to Fr. Ray Ball and All Saints Episcopal Church for accepting Doug and me into their fellowship and patiently listening to our ramblings and questions as we sorted through our beliefs and under-standing of God. To Debbie Thurman, author of multiple books and publisher at Cedar House Publishing, who asked to be a part of my team and who provided numerous pro bono hours, thank you for believing in me and mentoring me through this book process. I want to acknowledge my friends and family who encouraged this project, read drafts, and gave me their honest feedback: Joan Hand, Jean Smith, Donald and Mary Lou Langhorne, Sandy and Janet Buller, Butch and Donna Simon, Guy Duncan, Courtney Rindgen, Lu Vorghies, Jeanne Terrell, Mary Griffith, Carla Nix, and Sharron Fox. Also, a huge thank you to Sandra Holcombe for her editing skills and gift of encouragement. I am deeply grateful to Doug Crewse of Investigative Associates who guided me in the research into the background of Ole and was a constant source of encouragement throughout the writing and publishing process. And most of all, thanks to my best friend and husband, Doug, who encouraged me to write our love story. I cannot image life without you.

AUTHOR'S NOTE

This is my story and it undoubtedly suffers from my subjectivity. I have tried to portray my experience at Trinity Foundation in the most truthful and accurate way I could, drawing not only from my experience but also from the reflections of former members whose time at the foundation spanned the last thirty years. I contacted over three dozen former members of the Trinity Foundation and conducted over a dozen formal interviews. I directly quote only those former members who granted their consent. The names of all current and former members — except for Ole, Doug, me, and Crystal — have been changed to protect their privacy; Ole, because he is a public figure, Doug and me because this is our story, and Crystal because this book is dedicated to her and to her memory. Quotes from former members are the actual words they used, although in some instances they were edited for the purpose of space and clarity.

In addition to the informal and formal interviews from people associated with the Trinity Foundation, I spent hours listening to Trinity Foundation's tape recordings of Bible studies, which spanned the twenty of the last thirty years — they began recording their Bible studies in 1985. I poured countless hours into reading every newspaper or magazine article that could be found that had been written about Ole Anthony or the Trinity Foundation. I also invested months in researching Ole's background.

The dialogue used to tell this story came from former members and is not meant to be a verbatim account, since memory of specific words is often fleeting. However, I am confident that the substance of the dialogue is faithful to the actual events. People's memories were intense, especially in recalling the hot seats. In telling this story, I constructed dialogue collectively from parties who were present at the actual event. I was constantly amazed at the overlap and consistency in the accounts when I conducted independent interviews. There were very few times when there were significant variations in memory, and those events were not included in this story. There were many interesting recollections that I chose not to include because I was unable to obtain collaboration from another former member.

Many Christians have asked Doug and me if we have followed the process laid out in Matthew 18 to share our concerns with Trinity Foundation before going public with our story, as we are by publishing this book. For those who are not familiar with it, here is the passage to which they refer:

> If your brother sins against you, go and tell him his fault, between you and him alone. If he listens to you, you have gained your brother. But if he does not listen, take one or two others along with you, that every word may be confirmed by the evidence of two or three witnesses. If he refuses to listen to them, tell it to the church; and if he refuses to listen even to the church, let him be to you as a Gentile and a tax collector (Matthew 18:15–18, RSV).

In interpreting this scripture, it is helpful to examine the verses immediately prior to it in order to understand the wider context of the passage. Matthew 18:12–14 reads:

> What do you think? If a man has a hundred sheep, and one of them has gone astray, does he not leave the ninety-nine on the mountains and go in search of the

one that went astray? And if he finds it, truly, I say to you, he rejoices over it more than over the ninety-nine that never went astray. So it is not the will of my Father who is in heaven that one of these little ones should perish. (Matthew 18: 12–14, RSV).

Ole and Trinity Foundation have always maintained a policy, openly stated, that they do not chase "sheep"—in direct contradiction to the clear intent of the scripture. In fact, Trinity Foundation actively shuns its former members. When my husband, Doug, and I finally managed to break away from Trinity, we continued to live for four more months on the same block in east Dallas where they live, until we were able to sell our house and move. It was one of the most bizarre experiences of either of our lives, because it was as though we had suddenly become invisible. People whom we had known for years and thought were our friends abruptly quit talking to us and went out of their way to avoid us altogether—in spite of Doug's e-mail to one of the elders that we were available to meet with anyone who wanted to come over and discuss with us why we were leaving.

We offered to talk, we were willing to talk, but only one member took us up on it. One of the elders did tell Doug that he wanted him to come to Bible study and explain himself to the group, but Doug (rightly, I am certain) saw this as a ruse to get him on the hot seat (see chapter six). He discussed it with the therapist he was seeing at the time, and she advised him that he would be just setting himself up to be abused, and he agreed with her.

Much later, we were discussing this Matthew 18 issue with another former member, and he observed that if you do not feel safe to go to someone to discuss with them how they have offended you, then that person probably does not qualify as your brother. He has a point. I would not advise a friend of mine who was leaving an abusive husband that she was obligated to go meet with him to explain to him why she needs to leave. Once that sense of covering is broken it is broken, and the task for someone who has been abused is primarily to find a place to be safe and to heal.

This book was written for all the former members of this group and groups like it who have lost their way. I hope they can find hope and inspiration from my story, and see that, even after being involved in an abusive religious cult, there is a way back to psychological health, freedom, happiness, and, ultimately, even a way back to God.

CONTENTS

Prologue

"I can't hear God's voice anymore!" I shouted. "Your voice has gotten too loud!" I screamed at Ole Anthony, the leader of the Trinity Foundation, as I ran out of the room.

Earlier that morning in Bible study, Ole had chastised my boyfriend, Doug, for wanting to marry me. This was not the first time that Ole had rebuked Doug on the subject of marriage. It had happened on numerous occasions during the seven years we had been dating, but, for some reason, on that spring day of 2000, I could no longer tolerate Ole's manipulation. The proverbial light came on.

"Everything is perfect," Ole had told Doug. "If you think things are not as they should be, you are in a state of sin. You have to deal with your problem of self, Doug. Your evil self rises every time you think something should be different from the way that it is. God abhors self. Whenever your mind tells you that something should be different, you must ask God to forgive you. This has massive implications, as it destroys your propensity to want to be in control. You must repent from your sinful self-seeking immediately." In this manner, Ole persisted in deriding and verbally thrashing Doug for his desire to marry me.

The morning had started ordinarily enough. I was on a committee of the North Texas Council of Governments that was meeting that day in the nearby city of Arlington to

1

review grant applications submitted by local nonprofit organizations. As I dressed that morning, I smiled while thinking
of my friend Amanda who was also a member of the Trinity
Foundation. Amanda was a tall, attractive woman with a
strong personality. She and her husband, along with their
children, had joined the group before me. We had similar
religious backgrounds—she, too, had been a member of a
Baptist church before coming to the Trinity Foundation. Her
outspokenness always presented problems in her relationship
with the Trinity Foundation's leader, Ole Anthony, and its
elders. She had what the Trinity Foundation called a "rebellious spirit."

Amanda and I had recently discussed Trinity Foundation's
role in determining whether or not Doug and I could marry.
Doug had been a member of the Trinity Foundation for
twenty-one years and had been employed there for the last
eleven years. I was still considered a newcomer since I had
only been a member of the group for seven years, the length
of time that I had been dating Doug. We believed that we
were ready to marry, but we had yet to secure the approval of
the Trinity Foundation's leader, Ole Anthony.

"What right does Ole have to say when you and Doug get
married?" Amanda had asked me. I reminded her that, as the
leader of Trinity Foundation, Ole was our "spiritual covering," as were our Bible study teachers who were the elders of
the foundation. There were three Bible study groups at that
time. Amanda was in Ole's group and I was in the Bible study
my boyfriend co-led with a married couple, Jan and Garth
Brown. Another group was taught by Luke and Lee Ann,
who were also elders of the foundation.

"But you and Doug aren't kids, Wendy. You are both
in your forties, and you have been dating for seven years,"
Amanda pointed out. "I don't know if this spiritual covering
doctrine is right."

Trinity Foundation was infused with the concept of spiritual covering, though the group's actual teaching on the subject was somewhat vague. The Bible study teachers were considered the spiritual covering for the members of their Bible study group, just as Ole was the spiritual covering for the other teachers and, by extension, for the membership of Trinity Foundation as a whole. Though how much authority the leader was to exercise over his flock was not explicitly defined, it was understood that anyone contemplating a major life decision should discuss it with his "covering" and respectfully submit to the leader's wisdom and discernment in deciding how to proceed. Doubts or questions a member might have regarding his spiritual advice were seen as evidence that the individual was headstrong and self-willed—or had a problem trusting the leadership.

On many occasions since we had been dating, Doug had discussed the possibility of our marriage with Ole and the two elders with whom Doug taught in one of the Bible study groups. According to their spiritual discernment, Doug and I were not ready to be married. Ole's official position was that he did not control whether or not anyone married. He simply said whether or not the Trinity Foundation could bless the union and participate in the wedding ceremony; however, this was disingenuous. When he would say things to Doug like, "If you marry Wendy right now, it will be a disaster," he might as well have said, "I forbid it," but Ole was too subtle for that. It was more effective to claim that he had the spiritual insight to see that we were not ready to marry.

As I was pulling out of my driveway that fateful morning to go to my meeting in Arlington, I saw Doug walking down the sidewalk towards my car and I immediately sensed from his facial expression that something was wrong. I rolled down my car window and asked him what was going on. He explained that Amanda had asked Ole during her group's

Bible study the previous night where in scripture was the justification for the Trinity Foundation to control when and if members were allowed to marry. Ole apparently had stewed about her challenging question all night and had just attacked Doug publicly during the morning Bible study for his lack of contentment in being single.

That morning, for whatever reason, I could no longer tolerate Ole's manipulation. Although Doug begged me not to do so, I had to confront Ole. As I walked into the community dining room where Ole was eating breakfast, I was so angry that I could barely say hello to Hazel, Troy, and some of the other members who also were eating. I realized that what I was about to do was considered reprehensible behavior for a Trinity Foundation member. I knew that I was about to break one of the Trinity Foundation's unspoken rules: Do not challenge Ole—especially in public. I knew that what I was about to say was unacceptable in the minds of Ole and his followers—and would only be seen as evidence of my rebellious spirit—yet I proceeded.

"Ole, I need to talk with you," I said boldly.

"What is it?" he replied as he sat eating his breakfast of grapefruit and toast.

I was almost shaking with anger as I said, "I cannot continue to allow you to use the Bible and your teaching of the cross as a justification for Doug and me to remain single. You are twisting scriptural passages to convince us that it is a sin for us to want to marry. Your interpretation of scripture is not right, Ole."

"Wendy, your problem is that you have never understood the doctrine that we teach here at Trinity Foundation," he replied as he continued to eat, not even bothering to look at me.

"Ole, I do understand the doctrine. What I do not understand is why you will not give us your approval. We have been dating for seven years. We love each other. We are both believers."

"I don't give a rat's ass if you two get married!" he replied in a contemptuous tone.

"Then why do you keep opposing it?" I said. "Why do you persist in making Doug feel guilty for wanting to marry me? Your voice has gotten so loud, Ole, that I can't hear God's anymore!" I turned, ran out of the dining room, and drove away in my car.

I had never been so infuriated in my entire life or so confrontational, but as I drove through Dallas my anger dissipated, and I began to have a sinking feeling.

What on earth have I done? How could I have talked to Ole that way? I cried, believing that I had just lost the love of my life. *Doug will never be able to forgive me for my blatant and shameless rebellion against Ole, and Ole will never let me forget it.*

CHAPTER 1

✝

I Never Meant to Join a Cult

How had I given up one of my most basic freedoms—the right to choose a marriage partner—and turned over control of my life to a religious community? Why had I allowed myself even to become involved in such a group, where my personal liberty was compromised?

I never meant to join a cult. I was a Christian—a Southern Baptist. I had a post-graduate degree from a theological seminary, for goodness' sake. Cults were groups, such as Heaven's Gate, the People's Temple, or the Branch Davidians, whose sensational stories came to my attention through the media. Cult members were people you witnessed to about the true God—individuals you prayed for.

After leaving the religious community of which I was a member for seven years, I read cult literature and was disturbed by the similarities between my group and the ones characterized as cults by the experts in this field. I also read numerous memoirs by former cult members, and I saw my story in theirs.

There are many types of cults: political, religious, New Age, psychological, transformational, to mention a few, but what they share in common is best described in the definition provided by Michael Langone, executive director of the International Cultic Studies Association (formerly American Family Foundation), in *Recovery from Cults*:

> A cult is a group or movement that, to a significant degree, (a) exhibits great or excessive devotion or dedication to some person, idea, or thing, (b) uses a thought-reform program to persuade, control, and socialize members (i.e., to integrate them into the group's unique pattern of relationships, beliefs, values, and practices), (c) systematically induces states of psychological dependency in members, (d) exploits members to advance the leadership's goals, and (e) causes psychological harm to members, their families, and the community. [1]

The common denominator of all cultic groups is some form of excessive authoritarianism. However, as Dr. Langone points out in *Recovery from Cults*, organizations such as the military are different from cults in that the authoritarian structure is explicitly stated and there is accountability to an authority outside of the group. [2] Cults exist on a continuum, with some being more extreme than others. At one end of the spectrum are those that do tremendous damage to their members, and at the other end are some that are relatively innocuous. The group in which I was involved, the Trinity Foundation, located in Dallas, Texas, is not as extreme as the People's Temple or the Branch Davidians, and thus may appear to be benign, but the testimony of the dozens of former members I have interviewed shows that it is far from harmless.

The term *cult* is pejorative, and there is some subjectivity as to which groups can properly be categorized as such. Although practically everyone would concede that, for example, the People's Temple was a cult, there are some groups about which it is debatable whether the term should be used. "Sure, they are authoritarian, but the abuse does not rise to the level to earn the label," one might argue. However, based on both my personal experience and my extensive study of the literature in the years since I left the group, it is my opinion that the moniker can properly be applied to Trinity Foundation. The reader will have to draw his own conclusions.

Dr. Margaret Singer, a clinical psychologist who studied cults and thought reform since the 1950s, states in her book, *Cults in Our Midst*: "The term *cult* tends to imply something weird, something other than normal, something that is not us. But . . . cults are far from marginal, and those who join them are no different from you or me. The issues they represent are basic to our society, to our understanding of each other, and to our accepting our vulnerabilities and the potential for abuse within our world."[3]

In another chapter, Dr. Singer writes, "Despite the myth that normal people don't get sucked into cults, it has become clear over the years that everyone is susceptible to the lure of these master manipulators. In fact, the majority of adolescents and adults in cults come from middle-class backgrounds, are fairly well educated, and are not seriously disturbed prior to joining."[4] Dr. Singer believed that no one was immune to the influence of a cult if the person was introduced at a vulnerable time in his or her life. In retrospect, I proved to be particularly susceptible.

I grew up in a Southern Baptist home with Christian parents who were very much involved in the church. My father was a deacon and my mother held various leadership positions, including director of the Women's Mission Union (WMU). My parents took my baby brother, my three older sisters, and me to church several times a week. I became a believer at a very early age, but when I was ten years old, my family's faith in God was deeply tested. My father, a south Texas cattle rancher, was thrown from the horse he was riding, and our family was never the same. Although there was not a mark on his body, his brain was severely damaged. He was rushed to a hospital in Houston where he remained in a coma for over thirty days. When he finally was released from the hospital to come home, he limped when he walked, his speech was slurred, and his handwriting was illegible. He was emotionally unstable and was on potent mind-altering medications. My father was scary. Home was scary. Home was not a source of security and comfort any longer.

My mother blamed God for destroying our family. It was years before she made peace with Him about my father's accident. She was a housewife with five children and had never worked outside the home. Suddenly, and without warning, she was forced to assume the role of the family breadwinner. She returned to college, finished her undergraduate degree, and became a public school teacher. My mother discovered that the world of academe provided a refuge from her family situation, so she continued her postgraduate education, eventually earning a master's degree in political science. My mother became so immersed in books and studying that she and my father seldom attended church anymore. Many years later, after I graduated from high school and left home, my parents became confirmed Roman Catholics and were again anchored in a church.

It was difficult to sustain faith and an ongoing commitment to God while living in a chaotic environment—especially with a mother who was angry with God. My oldest sister managed to graduate from high school early so she could move away to college. My twin sisters disengaged from the emotional pain through rebellious behavior. I assumed the role of family caretaker until I, too, could escape.

The summer following my graduation from high school, I moved to Houston and enrolled at the University of Houston.

The adjustment from a high school graduating class of fifty students to a large university with an enrollment of twenty thousand was overwhelming. Before long, I sought the comfort that drugs appeared to offer. Since the time of my dad's accident, I had longed to recapture the sense of security and protection that I had experienced as a small child. By the end of my freshman year of college, I left school and married with the dream of feeling safe again. Predictably, I married a man with emotional problems and the marriage lasted only three years.

After the divorce, I returned to college so that I could complete a degree and pursue a career in social work. During my last semester of college, I had a profound experience with God and renewed my faith in Him. I had actually become a Christian when I was six years old, but like so many childhood conversions, it never matured into a deep relationship with God. My first encounter with God as an adult was powerful and undeniably real.

The joy of my renewed relationship with God was indescribable. The memory of that powerful experience kept me connected to God through many difficult times when I almost lost my faith. Even though I had taken an initial step towards God when I was six years old, my experience as an adult was one of those life-changing events. For the first time I saw God as a personal Being, and I was in awe that the God who created this universe, who breathed life into existence, could care about me, a woman so totally unworthy of His love. The wonder of this kind of love was incredible and inconceivable!

As a child, I had become a Christian to avoid hell and damnation. As an adult, my desire now was to know this God who had touched my life in an amazing way. My life changed radically. My commitment to living the life of a believer was so great that I broke off a relationship with a man who was my closest friend, and my first real love, because he was not a

Christian. I became engrossed in studying the Bible, reading Christian literature, and attending a Southern Baptist church. After several months, I became convinced that God was calling me into the ministry—specifically, foreign missions.

Because I had spent so many years away from the church, and because I was perhaps naïve, I did not realize that my divorce would be an obstacle to a life in the ministry of a Southern Baptist church. I thought that because I loved the Lord and wanted to serve Him that it was just a matter of preparing myself spiritually and vocationally. I did not realize that my divorce would be an impediment to my pursuit of what I felt was God's will. Neither did I realize how it would impact my feelings of acceptance in the church body.

At that time, I was attending a Southern Baptist church in Houston, and when I met with the pastor to tell him that I felt God had called me to the ministry, his reaction was, "Oh, hon, you can't do that. You have been divorced. This church cannot recommend you for seminary training." I was crushed and bewildered. I was certain that God had called me to serve Him, and my understanding of what a call to ministry meant was a full-time Christian vocation. I did not realize that God calls all believers to serve Him in whatever life situation or vocation they are in. All I felt then was a sense of rejection by mainstream Christianity and of inferiority to other believers that was to become an ever-present feeling through the next decade of my life.

After my pastor's assertion that the church could not recommend me, a requirement in the seminary application process, I pursued my previous goal of becoming a social worker. I began my first job in the social work field with the Texas Department of Human Resources. I loved the job, which was with the Emergency Family Services unit, and I found working with families in crisis to be personally fulfilling. My supervisor, Mary Barnes, was an excellent social worker and mentor. To this day, we still stay in touch.

Life was mostly good, except that I was lonely much of the time. Before I made my commitment to God, I had many friends and I had always had a boyfriend; however, since I began my relationship with God as an adult, I found it difficult to connect with other believers because I was self-conscious about my divorce. Since the time that I had started dating at age sixteen, a week rarely went by when I did not go out at least once. However, when I became involved with a church and renewed my relationship with God, I did not have a date for six years. This was not because I turned any down, I simply was not asked. Consequently, my dormant social life gave me more time to study the Bible and to read Christian books.

My desire to attend seminary never diminished, and periodically I met with my pastor to discuss it. Either he got tired of my persistence or God changed his mind, because a year later during a church business meeting, he asked the members if they would support my application to seminary. The church voted unanimously to provide a letter of recommendation.

The next hurdle was persuading the Admissions Board of Southwestern Baptist Theological Seminary in Fort Worth to consider the application of a divorced person. Through a long and emotional process, I was finally accepted, and I moved to Fort Worth to start seminary study.

Attending seminary was the highlight of my life. The joys of being surrounded by people who loved God and were committed to Him—along with the theological studies—were like nothing I had previously experienced. Without a doubt, the greatest reward of my seminary days was meeting Faith Smith and Mary Griffith, who became my closest friends and who provided much support and encouragement.

The only negative aspect was my intense humiliation at having been divorced. I desperately wanted to be like the other students and serve in the ministry without the disgrace associated with my past divorce. There was no way to undo the past, and I felt that I could never measure up — never be as spiritual and Christlike as my classmates. Only a handful of people knew my deep, dark secret.

During my last year of seminary, I finally realized that the dream of being a foreign missionary was unachievable. The Foreign Mission Board of the Southern Baptist denomination had stringent criteria for their missionaries and a history of divorce precluded me from the admissions process.

I then explored other mainstream evangelical mission boards and wrote one letter after another to various mission organizations; however, all my inquiries met with similar responses:

"I am sorry I must inform you that one of the rules of our denomination is that we cannot accept applications from divorced persons." And another: "While we appreciate your desire to serve the Lord overseas, it is not our policy to accept divorced candidates." Over and over, I received similar responses in my quest to become a missionary under other denominational mission boards. "It has been a long standing policy of our mission agency that we do not accept applications from divorced persons." And, "We do not consider divorced persons for missionary service."

Each response to a letter I had written confirmed in my mind that I was not good enough — that because of my previous divorce I was forever tainted in the eyes of my fellow Christians and my church.

After my graduation from seminary, I abandoned my dream of becoming a missionary and soon dated a minister. Our two-year relationship ended when I realized that he never saw marriage in our future. Several months later, he married another woman, leaving me once again with that familiar feeling of rejection. A year later, I met an attorney who proposed on our second date, and I readily accepted.

It was not surprising in hindsight that my need to feel loved and accepted would supersede any concerns about this relationship.

My second marriage was disastrous, and after three years, I could not endure the emotional and verbal abuse any longer. The shame of experiencing another divorce caused me to remain separated from my husband for eighteen months before we finally filed the legal paperwork to end the marriage. If one divorce made me defective in the eyes of my fellow believers, how would two failed marriages make me look? How would I ever be able to explain to church members that a person who claimed to be a Christian who loved God could commit the sin of divorce twice?

It was during this subsequent divorce that I met Doug and then attended Bible studies at the Trinity Foundation. I had an apartment in Fort Worth fifty miles west of the area in Dallas where Doug lived. In March 1993, we both happened to be in Austin, Texas, at a workshop on applying for grants to provide services to homeless persons. A meal was prepared for the attendees at lunchtime, and I sat down at the table where he and another member of the Trinity Foundation were eating. As was typical in those situations, we talked about the kind of work we were involved in and our purpose for attending the workshop. I explained that I worked for a community mental health center in Fort Worth and held the position of director for homeless and criminal justice programs for persons with mental illness. Doug, in turn, commented that he worked for a nonprofit organization in Dallas, the Trinity Foundation, a religious community that provided housing to persons who had no place to live. According to Doug, the Trinity Foundation was a community comprised of believers who were committed to living in the same fashion as first-century Christians. The majority of the members lived in a two-block area in east Dallas, homeschooled the children of the members, and functioned as a big family. They were committed to helping the homeless by actually taking them into their homes and providing a community of love and support.

In a moment of openness, I discussed that I was looking for a church, and Doug invited me to attend their Sunday evening dinner and Bible study. The dinner, he explained, was more like a potluck supper where everyone sat around the table in family style. We exchanged business cards, which led to the beginning of a friendship — and eventually — a dating relationship.

I grew up in a rural setting where everyone knew each other. I lived in the same house for eighteen years until I moved to Houston to go to college. From the time I was eighteen until I discovered the Trinity Foundation, I lived in no less than fifteen different apartments or houses. I had been a member of six different churches and, at the time I became familiar with Trinity, I was in the process of finding a church home. When Doug told me about the religious group that he belonged to, I decided to visit and was deeply impressed with the feeling of community that I sensed and observed among the members. For idealistic individuals, Trinity Foundation offered a place of hope and faith.

I never meant to join a cult. I was initially very skeptical; in fact, after I met Doug and he told me about the Trinity Foundation, I made some inquiries about the organization. I was not totally naïve. I knew that cults existed, and I had even taken a course on cults while I was in seminary. Before I attended my first Bible study at the Trinity Foundation, I called their main office and asked for information concerning their doctrinal beliefs and practices. When I received the pamphlets and reviewed them, they appeared to represent mainstream Christian beliefs. I also called several organizations, such as Probe Ministries, Interfaith Witness, Watchman Fellowship, and Christian Research Institute. These were all groups that served as resources for information about cults, and I asked their representatives if they had any reason to believe that the Trinity Foundation in Dallas was a cult. All of these organizations were familiar with the Trinity Foundation, but they did not classify it as a cult.

During the years after I graduated from seminary, I struggled to hold on to a close relationship with God, but the feelings of rejection associated with not being accepted by the Foreign Mission Board, and then the failed relationship with a Baptist minister, made me feel like I was not the kind of person with whom God wanted to have an intimate relationship. While I was separated from my second husband, I made an appointment with a Christian counselor, Buddy Westbrook, and told him, "I want my relationship with God back." Buddy was an excellent counselor and helped me reconnect to God.

It was during this time period when I was in counseling that I met Doug and asked Buddy if he had heard of the Trinity Foundation. Much to my surprise, he had. Several years prior, Buddy's daughter had a friend whose mother was dating Ole Anthony. Buddy told me that he had checked into Trinity Foundation then and determined that, while it was an offbeat type of organization, it did not appear to be a cult.

Reassured by my therapist, the cult awareness organizations, and through my own examination of their doctrine that the Trinity Foundation was not seen as a cult, I began attending its Bible studies and worship services.

I had not become a part of another church since my broken relationship with a minister. The Trinity Foundation offered me the possibility that I had stumbled into a genuine community of believers. When Doug talked about the Trinity Foundation, I had a glimmer of hope that, out there, somewhere, God's people were being who He wanted them to be. That hope, however, was mixed with doubt and apprehension. Part of me sensed that there might be something doctrinally unsound.

So, if I had these doubts about this group, what changed? I remember clearly the first time that I went to the Trinity Foundation's meetings. On Sundays, each of the Bible study groups met separately for what they called the Seder meal. This was the weekly celebration of the Sabbath and was one of the customs found in the Jewish tradition. Each member of the Bible study group would bring a covered dish, and everyone would sit around a big table in order of age. Before the meal could begin, the Seder leader would ask, "Does anyone have anything to talk about? Is everybody at peace with one another?" At this point, one of the members might ask permission to be excused to talk with one of the other brethren. The Seder leader always reminded the group that before the Seder meal could be eaten, everyone had to be in one accord. This meant that if anyone had a conflict with one of his or her spiritual brothers or sisters of the Trinity Foundation, it had to be resolved before the meal could begin. The reason we came together was to celebrate God's deliverance of the Israelite people and we could not celebrate until all leaven was destroyed. Leaven was described as anything — an opinion, judgment, or thought — that corrupted your peace or relationship with God or your fellow believer.

After individual members settled any problem that they may have had with one another, they would return to the group and the Seder meal. The second part of the ceremony would be the lighting of the candle by one of the women in the group. Only a female could light the Seder candle because it was a woman, Mary, who brought the light — Christ — into the world. After the candle was lit, the group pronounced the blessing and members toasted with a sip from the cup of wine. There were about fifteen people in my group, ranging in age from early twenties to early sixties. While some members were single, others were married. The group was comprised of individuals who had been homeless or drug addicts before coming to the Trinity Foundation, as well as individuals who were from middle-class backgrounds. There was indeed an eclectic mix with a wide range of educational, religious, and socioeconomic backgrounds. We had a great time talking and eating. After the meal, we cleaned up the dishes, and everyone then proceeded to "Big Group," where all the members met together for worship on Sunday evenings.

During Big Group there was singing, Bible study, taking of the afikomen, and drinking of a cup of wine. The afikomen was a piece of matzah (unleavened bread) that represented Christ's body, which was broken in death. At the Last Supper, the last meal Jesus had with his disciples, he took the afikomen, blessed it, broke it, and distributed it to his followers. Likewise, the afikomen was blessed, broken, and distributed to Ole's followers. After the afikomen, the cup of wine was blessed and passed around to the members.

The whole experience was captivating, and everyone was extremely nice and down-to-earth. I felt at home and accepted. Interestingly, four of the seven elders of the Trinity Foundation had belonged to Southern Baptist churches before joining Ole's group. Several people had graduated from Christian colleges, and one was even employed by the *Baptist Standard*, the weekly newspaper for Texas Baptists. With so many of the members having roots in the Southern Baptist denomination, it created a false sense of security that, although the Trinity Foundation was hardly conventional, it was not a cult.

The first part of the evening was spent singing. There were several musicians who comprised the Trinity band and played the piano, acoustical guitar, bass, flute, drums, and other instruments. The music and lyrics were created specifically for the Trinity Foundation by the band's leader and was some of the most beautiful Christian music that I had ever heard. I distinctly remember one of the songs we sang, *Heart Music*, which was about a new song, a song we could not hear before—before we came to the Trinity Foundation was the implication—and how all the words of love that we now had for one another were real. It was a beautiful and emotionally moving song. After we finished singing, Ole began teaching. I do not remember what he preached about that night, but I was impressed by how engaging and passionate he was and how welcome he made me feel.

When I started attending the Trinity Foundation, I did not curse or smoke, drank alcohol on only rare occasions, and did not watch risqué movies. The religious world that I had been a part of did not see those behaviors as acceptable for committed Christians. I read my Bible and set aside regular "quiet times" with God for prayer. At the Trinity Foundation, no one cared that I had been twice divorced. Many of its members had also experienced failed marriages. Many of them did not come from religious backgrounds, and this was their first exposure to "God stuff." Ole taught that abstaining from the "do nots" of mainstream Christian beliefs was pharisaical and legalistic. Influenced by Ole's belief system, a permissive culture existed at the Trinity Foundation, where irreverence was the norm. People told dirty jokes, made sexual innuendos, and profanity was openly and widely expressed—even in the Bible studies and by the elders. My desire for acceptance overrode concerns I initially had, and eventually I became desensitized to the crude language and behavior that was characteristic of the group.

Interestingly enough, after being in churches and among Christians where I never felt good enough, I was now becoming involved in a group where they thought I was too good—too religious. In fact, I was often ridiculed and called a Pharisee. For the first time in my adult Christian life, though, I did not feel like a stepchild. I believed I had finally found a place to belong.

This strong need to fit in, to belong, to be accepted for who I was, with all my past sins, apparently was stronger than my misgivings about Trinity Foundation's doctrine. During my early years of involvement with the group, there were numerous occasions where I would come home from a Bible study and examine for myself the doctrine that Ole was teaching at Trinity Foundation. I had a large library of reference materials, which included various translations of the Bible, and I would take out my seminary books on systematic theology and my *Strong's Concordance* so I could do a scripture search and look up the original word in Greek or Hebrew to figure out whether Ole's doctrine was correct. I always came away from my personal study realizing that what Ole taught was in error.

Also, early in our relationship, Doug and I had many theological discussions and arguments. He was very intelligent, extremely articulate, and knew the Trinity Foundation doctrine well. I recall one evening during one of our debates that I ended up in tears. I told Doug that I had nearly lost my faith in God after my seminary days and I had fought too hard to hang on to my belief in a loving God. Somehow, I instinctively knew that an acceptance of the doctrine taught by Ole would put my understanding of God at risk.

However, I also was — for the first time in my life — falling in love with a man who was genuinely committed to Christ. I had prayed for a man like Doug since I was twenty-five years old. In my ignorance, I thought I could keep my relationship with God intact and I could have a relationship with this wonderful man who had become the love of my life. Many times in Bible studies at Trinity Foundation, I would think to myself, "I don't believe what they believe." I learned early on if I said anything out loud I would be mentally and emotionally beaten into submission. However, slowly, over a period of time, my belief system was dismantled. The cognitive dissonance became too great and I eventually adopted Trinity Foundation's doctrine.

CHAPTER 2

✝

Doug's Story

Doug never meant to join a cult either. He met Ole Anthony when he was eighteen years old, during the summer following his high school graduation. For many people, graduating from high school is an unsettling time, and this was true for Doug. Although his future appeared promising, it was also unknown and, in some respects, intimidating. Friends that he had known in school were leaving to go their separate ways. Doug was planning to attend college at the University of Texas in Austin in the fall, and he was struggling with the same questions that most people at that stage of development ask: Can I measure up? Will I be able to make it on my own? What if I fail? Will I be able to make new friends?

Doug's best friend, Mark, had recently started attending Ole's Bible studies. At that time, Ole was in his 30s and, according to his own account, had been a millionaire businessman, a government spy, and a Republican candidate for the Texas legislature who had undergone a religious awakening in 1972.

It was while Mark was attending college in East Texas and teaching a Bible study for other college students that he first met Ole. One of the young women in the class related to Mark that she had attended a Bible study in Dallas taught by a man named Ole Anthony. She thought there was something odd about his teaching, but she could not put her finger on exactly what the problem was. Ole was so mesmerizing that she had become confused about whether or not what he was teaching was biblically accurate. She asked Mark to go with her to one of Ole's groups to help her determine whether his theology was doctrinally sound. When Mark attended Ole's Bible study, he was incredibly impressed. "I had never met anyone quite like him. Never met anyone as intelligent, erudite, and charismatic," said Mark. In this first encounter with Ole, Mark was intrigued with this man who claimed that he had been to the Promised Land and that he would show Mark the way. Ole's claim to understand the mysteries of God was very appealing to a young college student who was searching for the meaning of life.

After many discussions with Doug about this extraordinary new teacher he had discovered, Mark convinced him that he must also become acquainted with this man "whose theology was flawless." Doug finally agreed to meet Ole, and two days before Doug left for college, Mark introduced him to the eccentric Mr. Anthony.

Although it was over twenty years ago, Doug still remembers his first conversation with Ole. During their initial discussion Ole stated, "The biggest lie of modern Christianity is the idea of spiritual growth. Any effort on our part to become more like Christ is utter sin — for it is self-effort and God abhors the self. Trying to be a good Christian (reading your Bible, praying more, etc.) by your own self-efforts is pure vanity."

Ole's basic doctrine, or at least part of it, was the futility of trying to live the Christian life by principles. This was in sharp contrast to the evangelical Christian ministry, Young

Life, with which Doug was actively involved during his high school days. This nondenominational ministry to teenagers primarily focused on introducing adolescents to Christ, as well as teaching them to practice godly principles for living. With weekly Bible studies and youth activities, Young Life encouraged high school-aged kids to grow in their faith by developing the spiritual disciplines of Bible study, Christian fellowship, and prayer.

After meeting with Ole, Doug went home and studied several passages of scripture that he thought contradicted everything Ole had said. "I left my encounter with Ole and did some biblical research. I read Psalm 19, which described the precepts of God as being good, and I thought I had found the Bible verse proving that Ole was wrong," said Doug. With some assurance in hand, but doubts beginning to surface, Doug left for college and began his freshman year at the University of Texas in Austin. Once on campus, Doug attended Bible studies with the Navigators, an interdenominational, evangelical Christian group similar to Young Life, but with a focus on college students. The doubts that Ole had planted in his mind, however, continued to plague him.

When Doug returned home from college the following summer, he discovered that Mark had withdrawn from college, moved back to Dallas, and was exclusively attending Ole's group. Mark convinced Doug that he needed to attend at least one more Bible study at the Trinity Foundation. Mark persuaded Doug that even though he had looked up some scriptures that he thought contradicted Ole's doctrine, Doug still needed to meet with him one more time. "Intellectual honesty demands that you talk with Ole again," was Mark's rationale.

Doug attended one of Ole's groups, and afterwards they went to a coffee shop. Doug remembers that he had scriptures written out and that he and Ole had an extensive debate about them. Ole was extremely passionate in the way that he argued. He knew the scriptures, and his facility for recalling scripture verses was phenomenal.

"Even after all these years, I can still remember what Ole said that evening," Doug said, "and that was, how could God possibly be a God of love? Why would God love me more than the starving child in Africa? I had this overwhelming sense that Ole had given me a gift of divine enlightenment. In the blink of a moment I now saw that all the things that I was doing, like getting up early every morning to spend time in prayer and Bible study and slaving at being a good Christian, merely constituted trying to keep the law and trying to earn God's favor by my own efforts. I knew that salvation was unmerited grace, so why was I working so hard at it? It was mind-blowing."

Ole, a master manipulator, had tapped into a near-universal human vulnerability. Most people, because of their resident existential guilt, are always trying to earn merit with God and measure up to some ideal human standard. To offer someone a way around this exhausting—but unavoidable—struggle is very appealing. When someone can do this in the name of God, it is compelling and irresistible.

Twenty years after this second meeting with Ole, Doug reflected, "There was no way at that stage of my life with my intellectual development—completion of my freshman year of college—that I was going to win the debate with Ole Anthony on the scriptures. I was eighteen years old and way out of my league with Ole, who was thirty-eight at the time. Ole had been all over the world. He told us that he had run for public office, worked as a spy for the Defense Intelligence Agency, and had even started his own business. Although I had been involved with the Navigators and Young Life and had expended a considerable amount of time in reading and studying the Bible, in the contest with Ole, I was like a boy playing basketball with Michael Jordan. Put a basketball in the hands of a college kid and tell him to go play one-on-one with Michael Jordan, and he's going to get slam-dunked every time.

"I was also fascinated by the people who attended Ole's Bible studies. I grew up in middle-class America, in what Ole disparagingly called 'Ozzie-and-Harriet Land.' Attending these Bible studies was a group of people from all walks of life. There were many bright, young college students and professionals just getting started in their careers, but there were also people who were struggling with addictions, who had grown up in culturally and economically deprived environments. The folks who attended Ole's group were intriguing—a whole spectrum of society to which I had had little exposure. The interactions between group members, not to mention the tales of their escapades was, in many respects, like a living soap opera. I had never been to a Bible study where people talked about sexual affairs they were having and where swearing and foul language were the norm. At times, people would even start screaming at each other and fights would break out. It was actually pretty exciting!

"My plan was to go back to college in the fall, but Ole was subtly pressuring me not to return. My mother became very upset because she felt that I had become involved in a cultic group. She begged and pleaded with me to go back to college in Austin, and I ultimately did. I rekindled my involvement with the Navigators, but the wind had been taken out of my sails. I was questioning everything. It was like two competing systems that canceled each other out, and when I was at either one of them, the other one seemed wrong," said Doug.

The Navigators comprised a mainstream evangelical Christian group that placed a great deal of emphasis on the Bible and memorizing scriptures. Ole's teaching was, "If you are truly a believer, God will meet all of your needs without any effort on your part. You don't have to strive, struggle, or be concerned with your own spiritual growth in any dimension."

"The lilies of the field, the fowls of the air … are you not more precious than they are?" was a verse from the Bible that Ole liked to quote in order to prove to his followers that God did not require anything from the believer. Ole taught an extreme passivity with respect to the Christian life. On the other hand, the doctrine of the Navigators was that sanctification did require effort from man. Sanctification was the process a Christian was to undergo to become more like Jesus. In Doug's words, "I can't do justice explaining it, but it was not just different from that of the Navigators. It was the polar opposite, and only one of those two systems could be right."

During his sophomore year in college, Doug vacillated between the Navigators and the Trinity Foundation, but he was never the same after his encounter with the persuasive Ole Anthony. "I just felt that I was going through the motions with the Navigators," said Doug. "Whatever argument that either side could come up with, the other side had a counter-argument. I was in the Navigators, but I was very troubled by the things that Ole had told me, and his challenging questions continued to confuse me," Doug recalled.

Doug, like many young people at this transitional stage of life, was attempting to separate from his parents and their value system and to adopt his own set of values. Faced with the tasks of developing new friendships, discovering who he was apart from his parents, and developing a unique self-identity, Doug struggled with the universal—but still difficult—set of life challenges associated with entering young adulthood. This period is usually the first in an individual's life where he has a real taste of freedom, and suddenly he is faced with being responsible for day-to-day decisions. There are, moreover, the complex issues of having to decide on a college major and, ultimately, a career that combine to make this one of the most difficult times in a young person's life. Many young people also have a burning desire to arrive at some settled place about moral and religious values, which can seem like a daunting and overwhelming task.

As a college student, Doug experienced a lost sense of identity. He was extremely idealistic and curious, but at the same time, he longed for acceptance and a sense of belonging. In high school, he had been popular and was president of his class one year. He had a reputation for his intellect and quick wit. During his high school days, he knew most of his fellow students and enjoyed an esteemed role; now, enrolled in a university with fifty thousand students, he faced the task of distinguishing himself and redefining his sense of who he was. His conversations with Ole, which had created doubts in his mind regarding the reality of his relationship with Christ, continued to gnaw at him. Confusion between Ole's doctrine and that of the Navigators eventually became so great that he put his search for God on hold and became—in his own words—"almost agnostic."

During this "agnostic" period, Doug dated a young woman named Moira. Moira was raised in a home environment completely opposite from Doug's "Ozzie and Harriet" middle-class lifestyle. Her father left when she was six weeks old, which forced her uneducated, unskilled mother to provide for herself and her child. Money was tight, and many of the basic needs of love and nurturing a young child were set aside in the attempt to meet the essentials of food and shelter. When Moira was five, her mother met and married a man who proved to be an abusive alcoholic, and Moira spent the remaining years of her childhood and adolescence in a chaotic, tumultuous environment. Her stepfather abandoned the family when Moira was thirteen, and her mother faced the challenge of raising her two children alone. Moira was anxious to be rescued from her home life, and when she was eighteen she met Doug, who became her "knight in shining armor"—someone who would love and care for her and provide her with the security that she so desperately desired.

Having someone who so desperately needs you can be intoxicating, and Doug, in his search for his own identity, was more than willing to assume the role of caretaker for this needy and emotionally neglected young woman; however, the church teaching that Doug had been exposed to clearly stated that Christians were not to marry unbelievers. Doug consequently shared the "plan of salvation" with Moira who prayed the "sinner's prayer," thus becoming a Christian. His next step was to get her involved with Bible study and he knew Ole's group, the Trinity Foundation, was the place she would best fit in—and she did.

Because both Moira's father and her stepfather abandoned the family, and because Moira's childhood was often unpredictable and unsettling, she was on a never-ending quest for male approval, which she found in the charismatic leader of the Trinity Foundation, Ole Anthony. Ole preached that at the Trinity Foundation one was "home." Fellow members were your brothers and sisters. The Trinity Foundation offered a place of belonging, of security, of never having to be alone. Moira was instantly attracted to this refuge and remembered Ole's teaching as, "Those people out there in the world are the individuals whom God sees as flesh, but they're not your family. This is your family. This is the Body of Christ."

Being a part of a loving, stable family was what Moira had been searching for all of her life and now, in the Trinity Foundation, she had found it. The concept of the family, as well as the other doctrines taught by Ole Anthony, was all extremely appealing to her. In Moira's words, "I was raised in a Catholic background. I had been a wild teenager, but when I went to the Trinity Foundation, Ole was preaching about freedom in Christ and the law being dead. Legalism and the ritualism observed by the Roman Catholic Church were not necessary. I latched on to that. I felt like, 'Hey, I don't have to feel guilty anymore.' I didn't have to feel sick to my stomach if I hadn't gone to confession before taking communion. There was liberty," she said.

That sense of freedom didn't last very long after she and Doug married. In five years, Moira gave birth to three children. With three small daughters, the demands of attending Ole's Bible studies three times a week, and the pressures of financial difficulties with a husband who was trying to finish college while holding down a job, Moira increasingly felt trapped. Her new ticket to freedom came a year later when she met Reuben, who had recently begun attending Trinity Foundation's Bible studies. Reuben was carefree, exciting, and offered an escape from the constant struggles of being in a marriage with a husband who was frequently away from home working or attending school, along with the daily frustrations of raising young children.

Shortly after meeting Reuben, Moira decided to take her daughters and move to Florida with him. After losing his wife and children, Doug was emotionally devastated. Ole and the group played an increasingly important role in his life. Ole and Doug discussed his becoming a Levite for the Trinity Foundation and Doug decided to do so, thinking it would give him an opportunity to take a break from the pressures of the work world and provide a time of healing from his divorce. The term Levite came from the Old Testament and referred to the descendants of Levi who were responsible for the care of the Tabernacle and its service. The concept of Levites had been introduced into the Trinity Foundation's social system about three years before Doug's divorce. The Levites at the Trinity Foundation had a variety of jobs, such as maintaining Trinity's physical plant, secretarial duties, and teaching in the small private school that Trinity had for the children of its members. Doug's function was as a teacher and Ole's aide-de-camp. Although Doug had originally planned to work for the Trinity Foundation as a Levite for only a short period, he continued in this role for the next eleven years, earning fifty dollars a week (in addition to having a place to live and meals from the community's diner). He and Ole shared the downstairs unit of one of the duplexes on the block, along with Kay, another Levite who worked as Ole's personal secretary and secretary for the Trinity Foundation.

Doug had been a member of the Trinity Foundation for over fourteen years when I met him, and he was committed to its stated mission and purpose. He served as one of the seven elders for the foundation and was on its board of directors. Early in my relationship with Doug, I realized that the Trinity Foundation was important to him and had resigned myself to the inescapable fact that it was more important than I was. I understood that it would always come first in our relationship and accepted that reality. Just as Doug had done, I think at some point, I, too, began to equate the Trinity Foundation with God.

Doug's undeniably strong bond with Ole, when I allowed myself to think about it, was disturbing. Ole appeared to have taken on the role of Doug's surrogate father—but one that was an authoritarian, abusive parental figure. Doug, at times, seemed like a young adolescent, incapable of making decisions for himself. Doug explained to me that when he became a Levite, he had given up the right to himself; therefore, in every situation he was required to seek Ole's approval before he could act. Even such decisions as when his children would be allowed to visit had to be cleared by Ole. Every aspect of his life was devoted to serving the community of Trinity Foundation and of course, Ole.

I, nevertheless, had fallen hopelessly in love with him and wanted to spend the rest of my life with him. And now, seven years after we had met, I thought that my relationship with this man who had become my best friend and the love of my life was over. My confrontation with Ole regarding his opposition to our desire to marry and his use of scripture to justify his position had created a situation that I feared would never be rectified.

CHAPTER 3

The Community

Imagine a place where you are accepted and loved, where there is complete honesty and transparency, where you can totally be yourself and no longer have to strive to be someone else. Envision a safe haven where you could live in perfect peace and have everything you needed and wanted. That was the dream — the hope — that Trinity Foundation offered and that we naïvely believed. We longed for a shelter from the fast-paced lifestyle that surrounded us; we yearned for a harbor of refuge from the stressful concerns of life. We had a vision of living in a community of people who aspired to be like Jesus and to live like the first-century Christians. For those of us who became a part of the group, there was also an intense hunger for spiritual guidance and religious truth, a hunger that was easily exploited.

For a brief time in our lives, we believed that we had found true community. We believed that we had found a special group of believers whose only desire in life was to become more and more like Christ. We believed that we were a people with a unique purpose in the kingdom of God and that we were a part of the glorious mystery of God. It was as though we had found a cocoon that would keep us safe from the world, a cocoon that would protect us from the afflictions of life. Not until years later did we come to know that a cocoon is something you are supposed to break out of.

When I first discovered the Trinity Foundation, I was full of joy that I had finally found a "church" where I could have a sense of belonging. The Trinity Foundation appeared to be a fellowship of believers who were committed to living similarly to the first Christians. The *block* was their affectionate term for their two-block community in east Dallas, and their concept of community—"holding all things in common" like the early church—was very appealing. I thought I had found a family of believers who were truly living as God desired.

I was also deeply impressed with the ministries of the foundation. At that time, I was working for a public community mental health center and directing a program for homeless people with mental illness. The agency where I was employed had been chosen to participate in a national research demonstration project and I was selected as the project leader for one of the two Texas sites. One of Trinity Foundation's missions was to help the homeless—not through the traditional social service approach—but by actually bringing homeless people into the community, providing them a place to live with one of its families, and genuinely embracing them.

My role as project director for the homeless program required frequent trips to Washington D.C., where I would meet with colleagues who were in charge of the research project in their respective states. After one of these trips, I decided to stop and see Doug while I was in Dallas. Doug was meeting with Ole and the elders when I arrived on the block and Ole asked me if I could babysit the children of a homeless mother who was staying in one of Trinity Foundation's apartments. The woman needed someone to take care of her four children while one of the Bible study members took her to the grocery store.

While babysitting these rambunctious, ragamuffin children, I was struck by the realization that only hours before I had been sitting at a conference table in my business suit with experts on homeless persons discussing the efficacy of the programs we had developed. The research demonstration project we were engaged in was designed to explore what program components—vocational training, assistance in accessing government entitlements, substance abuse treatment, etc.—were the key to solving the problems associated with homelessness. Now, literally hours after being in Washington, D.C., I was holding a homeless baby who smelled as if she had not had a bath in weeks, while watching her three siblings with their little dirt-caked faces and hands. Here was Trinity Foundation, with no expertise in this area, simply meeting the needs of one homeless family. That experience had a strong impact on me and increased my desire to be a part of such a remarkable circle of people.

Another of the foundation's ministries that impressed me was the investigations of prominent televangelists. Shortly before I became a member, the Trinity Foundation received national exposure for their work with Dianne Sawyer on ABC's *PrimeTime Live*. The results of its investigation of three nationally recognized televangelists, Robert Tilton, Larry Lea, and W. V. Grant, led to a great deal of media publicity about the Trinity Foundation and its charismatic leader, Ole Anthony. I was proud to be a part of a group that was supposedly exposing religious charlatans. The work of the foundation was significant and by virtue of my connection with them, I was important, too. There was a certain amount of euphoria in the feeling of being special—unique—and more righteous because I was a member of this extraordinary church which actually demonstrated its love for mankind and its disdain of hypocrisy.

From a sociological and psychological perspective, the development of the Trinity community is a fascinating study—an analysis, however, that is outside of the scope of this book. Even so, in order to have some understanding of the appeal of the group in the lives of people who became a part of it, some discussion of the elements that created its sense of community is essential.

When Trinity Foundation came into existence in the 1970s, its members lived in all areas of the Dallas/Fort Worth metroplex. In 1980 one of the married couples bought an old house in east Dallas and restored it. Four years later, a second family purchased another house on the very same block and renovated their home. As houses and duplexes became available, more and more of the members moved into this transitional neighborhood, which was located in the Junius Heights area of Old East Dallas, about three miles from downtown.

Built in the early 1900s, the original houses in this area were stately, two-story homes designed in the prairie-style architecture, which was common in that day. Following the Great Depression and World War II, however, the once-fashionable neighborhood fell into disrepair. Zoning laws were changed to allow multifamily dwellings, and most of those beautiful homes were converted to duplexes and rooming houses.

By the time I arrived in 1993, most of the members lived in old houses in various stages of renovation or in one of the condominium units across the street. The elegant houses with their wide front porches and balconies lined the street, which was graced with tall pecan trees, flowering crepe myrtles, and squirrels scampering on the lawns. The neighborhood stood in sharp contrast to the surrounding area of urban decay littered with pawn shops, rundown liquor stores, and dilapidated boarding houses. In spite of the ever-present sounds of gunfire and police sirens, the block somehow managed to exude an atmosphere of calm and peace.

The members of the Trinity Foundation comprised a diverse group drawn from a variety of socioeconomic backgrounds. There were professionals, blue-collar workers, and former homeless persons. Some were highly educated, while others barely had any schooling at all. There were single people, married couples, single mothers with children, and divorced or widowed persons.

Living in proximity to other members of the group provided numerous opportunities for frequent interaction and a greater sense of community. As in a small town where one knows everyone, the same was true of the Trinity Foundation—but to an even greater extent. Disclosure of one's feelings and personal affairs was encouraged, if not demanded. "You can't hide in a community," Ole would often say. "Everyone must bear each other's burdens. If one hurts, the whole "body" hurts with him," was another Ole saying. The Trinity community was a "boundaryless society" where few personal boundaries existed. Doors were rarely locked and people in the group walked in and out of each other's homes without knocking. If a married couple had an argument late at night, they thought nothing of going immediately to the home of one of the elders to seek spiritual counseling.

In the psychology literature, the concept of an "enmeshed family" refers to an extreme intensity and over-involvement in the family's interactions with one another. When a family is enmeshed, each person's identity is connected to the family as a whole with little sense of being a separate individual. In many respects, Trinity Foundation was like an enmeshed dysfunctional family. The overriding value was one of cohesiveness and bonds between members were tightly interwoven.

Personal boundaries were seen as detrimental to a people who were living in community.

Ole preached the "vow of poverty" as the overriding ideology of the group. In his conceptualization, the vow of poverty was not a declaration of destitution, but an affirmation of community. The vow was, "Whatever I have that you need to use, you can use. Whatever I own that you need to own, I'll give it to you. Whatever you need that I don't have, I'll help you get." The concept of true community meant that you gave up the right to control anything, the right to own anything, including your possessions, your time, and your very self.

In the Trinity Foundation's philosophy, the sense that one owns anything was contrary to a Christian community. One must always be willing to lay one's life down and to take no thought of oneself. Living in community was imperative for understanding the mysteries of God, for it was only in community, where one was constantly challenged by the needs of others, that a believer could truly live as God demanded. The daily choice of preferring to meet the needs of others, rather than one's own needs, caused us constantly to have to confront and repent from our own self-centered, sinful nature.

Shortly after I met Doug in 1993, I had moved from Fort Worth to Arlington, a city located between Fort Worth and Dallas. I purchased a small, two-story house and felt a sense of accomplishment that, as a single woman, I was able to afford a nice house in the suburbs. Being closer to Dallas also allowed more opportunities for Doug and me to see each other (since we only lived thirty miles apart, as opposed to the fifty miles when I lived in Fort Worth). During that time in our relationship, Doug would come to Arlington to visit on Friday or Saturday night and I would go into Dallas on Sunday for the Seder meal and worship service. Our relationship developed very slowly since we were only seeing each other twice a week.

Doug would often encourage me to think about moving to Dallas so that I could become more involved with the group. I only came on Sundays, and so I was not considered a full-fledged member. After two years of being on the periphery of the group, an apartment on the "block" became available and I decided to move there. I rented out my home in Arlington and moved into the upstairs apartment in one of the old houses that Trinity owned. Before I moved in, members renovated the apartment: the beautiful hardwood floors were restored, the walls were patched and painted, and new flooring was installed in the kitchen. This was a major change from the modern home where I had been living; however, the apartment in one of the old houses was filled with character and charm.

Since most of the members lived in the same area of where the Trinity Foundation had its offices, diner, Bible studies, and homeschool, it provided more opportunities to be involved in all aspects of semi-communal living. I loved living in the community. My apartment was above the Lair, which was the small restaurant that the group maintained so that its members could share their meals together. Members took turns serving the meals and washing the dishes, so there was continual activity going on. It was almost like living in a college dorm. Invariably, there were always people around, so that one never lacked for companionship. On Friday and Saturday nights, movies were shown on a large-screen television that Trinity Foundation had in a large open area of its offices.

Two significant events happened in the first week that I moved to the block. Across the hall from my upstairs apartment unit were two single-room apartments. One of the individuals in my Bible study group lived in one of the rooms. Leroy was a middle-aged, African American man who had been a homeless drug addict prior to joining the Trinity Foundation. Shortly after I moved in, Leroy asked if he could borrow my portable radio and cassette player and I agreed. A few days went by and on Sunday afternoon before my Bible study group was scheduled to meet, I had a phone call from my elders asking me to come to a meeting with Leroy. I quickly walked down the street to my Bible study teachers' home and was informed that Leroy had pawned my small stereo so he could buy some drugs. After his escapade, Leroy had confessed to our elders and now wanted to apologize to me. The stereo was relatively inexpensive, but my feelings were hurt. Leroy and I talked it through and I thought it was over. That evening in Big Group, Ole publicly reprimanded Leroy for betraying me, the newest member of the community, and he was not allowed to take communion with us. I felt sorry for Leroy, but at the same time, I felt protected and safe. "Ole will make sure nothing bad will happen to me," I thought.

The second significant event that further solidified my sense of community happened the first night at my new apartment when a little girl came to my door and announced that she was spending the night with me. There were a number of young children in the group, and because I did not have any children of my own, this was a special treat. I loved that there were so many children on the block, and that they immediately accepted me as someone important in their lives. At Trinity Foundation, the children were taught that all of the adults served as parental figures, so any need that they might have could be addressed with any of the older members. I often thought how fortunate the mothers of Trinity Foundation were — they did not have to cook meals for their families or any of the associated tasks of meal preparation, such as grocery shopping and cleaning up the dishes and kitchen. Plus, they had a host of free babysitters available if they wanted to run errands or to shop. Or if a child wanted to go somewhere and the mother was busy or simply did not feel like driving, the child had a number of adults who could help. This aspect of community was very appealing to married couples since it provided a tremendous amount of help in the normal pressures of raising children.

In addition to the support mentioned above, Trinity Foundation also provided a school for the children. One of the members, Lee Ann, had a degree in education from Baylor University and when the Trinity school was started, she became its director and primary teacher. Many of the adults had a variety of undergraduate and graduate degrees and they used their knowledge to teach some of the more specialized classes.

Two years after I moved into the apartment on the block, one of the houses on Columbia Avenue was offered for sale. I made a further commitment to the Trinity Foundation by becoming one of its home-owners. The house, which was built in 1915, had been converted into a duplex. Like the other two-story houses on the block, it had been designed with the high ceilings, hardwood floors, beveled windows, wide front porch, and balcony. I moved into the upstairs unit of the duplex and rented out the first-floor unit. Before I moved in, as was the custom, members came over to paint and help get it ready for occupancy. It was a wonderful, old house and I was thrilled with my new home. I loved living on the block and being part of the community. I felt that I was involved in a great and meaningful expression of Christianity. My whole sense of self was wrapped up in the mission of the Trinity Foundation and the lives of its members.

As a single woman living in an old home that was constantly in need of repair, I liked this concept of community. It meant that anytime my toilet overflowed or a bulb went out in one of the light fixtures on my twelve-foot ceilings, someone was available to meet my need. When I went out of town, there was somebody willing to water my plants and take care of my dog. Or if I was sick, there was always someone in the group who offered to bring me medicine from the pharmacy or food from the Trinity Foundation's dining room. As an independent person, it was always hard for me to ask for help, but at the Trinity Foundation asking for help was encouraged; indeed, failure to ask for help was seen as an affront to the whole concept of community.

One of the former members, Amanda, provided her initial impression about the group: "The promise of the community was one to which I had never been exposed. I came from Nebraska, where my family was all spread out, so the idea of a community was appealing to me. I liked the idea of having a circle of people with whom I could have genuine relationships.

"When my family and I started going to the Trinity Foundation, I was impressed by how friendly and helpful everyone was. My husband and I bought one of the old houses on the block and it needed a lot of work. Ole would declare a workday on Saturdays where everyone would come and help fix up the house. I felt a sense of security being a part of the community and a part of the body."

Not only was help available anytime you needed it, but there were also endless opportunities to socialize with other people. Anytime you had the need or desire to talk with someone, all you had to do was go outside your door. There was almost always another member or two outside on their porch or in their yard, or you could simply go to the dining hall where people often gathered. I do not ever recall experiencing loneliness when I lived on the block, in sharp contrast to my life prior to joining the Trinity Foundation.

Before moving to the block, I lived alone in a small house in Arlington. My Saturdays were spent cleaning my house, washing clothes, and doing all those weekend chores that busy, single people cannot seem to get done during the week. In the late afternoon, I ran errands and, in responding to a cashier or salesperson, I would hear my voice for the first time and realize that I had not spoken to anyone all day. It always seemed so odd that I could go almost a whole day without having any interaction with another person.

It was not that I had no friends, but most of them worked and had the same pressure to complete household chores and errands on the weekends that I did. Living in the sprawling Dallas/Fort Worth metroplex meant that most of the people I knew were scattered over a wide geographic area, and it would require at least a thirty-minute trip to reach their homes. Visiting with friends required some planning, setting up a time that was convenient for both parties and deciding what to do or where to meet. At the Trinity Foundation, however, spontaneity ruled. If you wanted to go to the movies or eat out, all you had to do was go outside your door, and you could usually find someone who was available. After Amanda left the group, she described Trinity Foundation as a "lazy man's social haven" because one did not have to expend any effort in order to have an immediate circle of "friends." She had a point. Most relationships in our society today take time and energy to develop. At the Trinity Foundation, members were in and out of each other's homes on a frequent basis. Because of the concept of community and the lack of real or perceived boundaries, you could have "instant" relationships.

The sense of our uniqueness as a community was reinforced by rituals that created a sense of elitism and separateness from the rest of Christendom. Ole taught that in AD 135 when the Roman Emperor Hadrian forbade *Torah* study, Jewish courts, Sabbath observation, and all Jewish ritual practices, the Christian church forsook the Jewish feasts, thus losing its Jewish roots and severing itself from the mystery of God. At Trinity Foundation, Ole restored the historic practice of celebrating these feasts. In Leviticus 23, God spoke to Moses and described the feasts that he wanted the Israelites to observe. According to Ole, the word *feast* meant the "set time" of the Lord, and such occasions were the only important days in our lives. In Ole's theological interpretation, God's commands regarding observations of the Old Testament feasts were still in force—and applied to Christians just as much as to Jews; of course, most Christian theologians would not agree.

Ole taught that Christ was revealed in the feasts, and every one who claimed to be a Christian celebrated the feasts during the first one hundred fifty years of the church. God desired His people to observe these religious holidays so that they could more clearly understand the meaning of Christ. In Ole's perspective, the celebration of the feasts was what kept the church (and before that, the Jewish community) from being mixed with the idolatry of the world.

Special emphasis was placed on the three pilgrimage feasts: Passover, Pentecost, and Tabernacles. The Feast of Passover revealed that the true Israel was betrothed as the Bride of Christ; during the Feast of Pentecost the Bride of Christ was empowered; and the Feast of Tabernacles was the wedding ceremony between Christ and his Bride, that is, the church. Other feasts observed by the Trinity Foundation were: Hanukkah, the Feast of Lights, which according to Ole, was when Christ was conceived by the Holy Spirit; Rosh Hashanah, which was when Christ was actually born; and Yom Kippur when Christ was baptized. Ole believed that one of his roles as leader of the community was to create a sense of excitement about the feasts—as well as a fear of not attending them. It was through keeping these religious festivals that God showed Ole and his followers more and more of the mystery of Christ. For the Jewish people, if you did not appear at the appointed time—particularly if you missed one of the pilgrimage feasts—you were "disfellowshipped" and shunned from the community. The Jewish people believed that Israel was the light of the nations, and thus, to be cast out of Israel into the Gentile world was the same as being thrown into spiritual darkness. Ole taught that the Jewish people did everything in their power to travel to the temple to be present with the Lord at the feasts. The observance of the feasts kept Israel from being assimilated into other cultures. Likewise, the feasts were a very special part of the culture of the Trinity Foundation and were important in strengthening the group's consciousness of being a unique people.

On the day of a major feast, Trinity members gathered in the morning and made preparations for the evening celebration. There were numerous tasks to complete before the actual feast occurred — the huge tent, which would serve as the dining and worship area, had to be set up; furniture had to be moved into the tent; dishes to wash; tables to set; linens to iron; and food to prepare. It was a labor-intensive effort to complete all the work by evening when the festivities would begin. Most of the feasts entailed a fast before the community gathered for a celebration, and so, in addition to the camaraderie associated with getting ready for the event, there was the common bond of getting through the hunger pains.

After all the preparations had been made, it was time for the feast. The interior of the tent was decorated with beautiful flowers and bathed in white materials to give the illusion of a temple. It was a sacred evening marked by a delicious meal, lots of wine, and a time of beautiful singing and worship. The feasts, moreover, served as important times to tie the community closer together.

Another important belief that was instrumental in developing a community with strong bonds to one another was Ole's concept of family. One's true family was not his biological family, but rather the other members of the group. The people of Trinity Foundation were brothers and sisters in Christ. In Ole's understanding of the Bible, the last Passover that Jesus observed was monumental because he did not eat the Passover with his blood relatives, but rather his new family—his followers. Until the third Passover of Christ's ministry, households celebrated the Passover together, but at the last Passover, before Jesus was crucified, He held it with His twelve disciples. At the last Passover, according to Ole, Jesus abolished "family values." When Jesus chose to have Passover with his disciples rather than with his nuclear family, He was sending a message to the early Christians that the church was the one true family.

At Trinity Foundation the clear message was that your biological family was not as important as the Trinity community. Furthermore, Ole taught that, in modern Christianity, the evangelical Christians taught family values, which was ridiculous from his perspective. According to Ole, if you searched the scriptures you would discover that the families mentioned in the Bible were the most dysfunctional that ever existed.

Ole credited the "Lair"—the communal dining room—with being the catalyst that transformed Trinity Foundation from a mere Bible study into a real community. Located on the first floor in one of the houses on the block, the Lair was where the members shared meals. The Lair came into existence at the time that Ole pronounced that the group would all take the "Nazarite vow." The word "Nazarite" in the Old Testament was used to indicate someone who was devoted wholly to God and separated from the world. This solemn oath taken during Old Testament times consisted of abstaining from wine or strong drink, avoiding contact with anything dead, and refraining from cutting one's hair. In biblical days, the vow was taken either for a short time period or for life, and was a reminder that God desired His people to live consecrated lives.

The Nazarite vow, which Ole's followers pledged, included a very restrictive diet: no meat, no sugar, very little fat, and no fruit of the vine because that fruit was used to make wine, and drinking wine was absolutely forbidden. Not only were the members to observe this very strict diet, but there was also to be no reading of newspapers, magazines, or any books apart from the Bible. Television, movies, and radio were not allowed, sex was taboo, and the cutting of one's hair or beard was not permitted during this time of consecration.

To ensure that the group adhered to all the requirements of the diet, Ole decided that meals would be prepared daily for the entire group. That was when the Lair was officially created.

In Ole's mind, the Nazarite vow is what caused his disciples to coalesce into a body, a true community. Although most of the members remember this three-month period as one of the most oppressive times during their experience at the Trinity Foundation, it resulted in the institution of the Lair, and was thus crucial in building the cohesive group that Ole wanted. Communal dining provided a time for the members to get to know each other better, to chat about the mundane things of life, and certainly strengthened the bond between individuals. In many respects, however, it weakened the fabric of the nuclear families in the community.

Breakfast time and the dinner hour provide family members with an opportunity to talk with one another and to catch up on what was happening in each other's lives. When the Lair came into being, it had the effect of distancing individuals within a family unit from one another and reinforcing the concept of the community as one's true family. Ole would ridicule married couples when he saw them eat together at the Lair. Amanda recalled that on one occasion, she and her husband were sitting together in the dining hall and Ole said in a mocking tone, "Oh, isn't that sweet. Amanda and Jake, the perfect little couple, sharing their evening meal together."

Another unique aspect of the Trinity Foundation, which further developed the community, was the institution of the "Levites." In the Old Testament days, the Levites were the tribe in Israel that was solely dedicated to the service of the temple. As such, they did not have a portion of the land designated for them to work and to use to meet their physical needs, as did the other tribes. The other tribes provided for them through tithes and offerings. The Levites were to be totally devoted to the service of the temple and were assistants to the priests. According to Ole, the Levites of the Trinity Foundation were a picture to the members of what the believer's true position was in Christ.

At Trinity Foundation, the Levites were the individuals who worked exclusively for the foundation. These individuals took a vow of poverty and served the needs of the community. Their compensation included a place to live and a meager amount—eighty dollars a week—from which thirty dollars was deducted to pay for their meals at the Lair. The Levites performed various jobs—some worked in the kitchen; some were responsible for landscaping or maintenance of the houses on the block; some taught in Trinity's school; and still others worked in the office or were involved in the investigations of the televangelists. Ole's conception and implementation of the Levites was a brilliant idea because it gave the foundation cheap labor in the name of performing service for the Lord. The Levites were at the beckoned call of Ole on a 24/7 basis, which was useful for the televangelist investigations when he needed people to go out in the middle of the night to do a trash run—which meant going through some ministry's trash looking for incriminating or embarrassing documents.

In the beginning of Trinity Foundation's history, Bible studies were held three or four times a week. Sometime in the late 1980s, Ole "laid hands" on five married couples and designated them as the elders for the community. They were charged with starting their own Bible study nucleus, and

Ole started a separate new one of his own, which became a new Seder group. One of the five couples never got a Bible study off the ground, but the other couples formed their own separate groups. The original disciple group that Ole started in the seventies was now primarily made up of the elders who met with him on Wednesday nights and who were considered the inner circle. On Sundays following their Seder meal and doctrinal study, the individual groups met as a whole for a weekly time of worship and taking communion. In addition to the evening meetings, the employees of the foundation (and anyone else who wanted to come) met every weekday morning over breakfast at the Lair for a lesson on Ole's theology before the workday began.

The structure for the fellowship groups included a discussion of any issues or problems a member was experiencing and then a time for study of Trinity's doctrine. Initially, I enjoyed attending the Bible studies with my group of eccentric members. The meetings were seldom dull, because inevitably someone would make a confession of wrongdoing, and then the whole time would be focused upon that individual. There was usually quite a bit of drama, and someone always ended up crying, or a big fight would break out and people would scream and yell. It was all very exciting—at least, in the beginning.

Although the common dining, semi-communal living, observation of the Jewish feasts, the sharing of lives, and the enormous amount of time spent in doctrinal study were all important in the development and maintenance of the Trinity community, the critical aspect in the success of the community was the teaching on the destruction of self-seeking and what it meant to "lay down your life." Using the passage of scripture from 1 John 3:16—"Hereby perceive we the love of God because he laid down his life for us: and we ought to lay down our lives for the brethren"—Ole taught that it was only in community that one could learn to lay down his life for the brethren and forsake all self-seeking. Only in community can God perform a purifying process on the believer. "The friction of the body is the greatest refining process that God has of teaching the believer to lay down his life," was Ole's explanation of why community was so important.

Ole believed that after the miracle at Pentecost which began the church age, God no longer dealt with people as individuals, but as members of a body. Therefore, to fully understand the mystery of God we had to realize that God did not deal with us as individuals, but as a body, as one people. No one seemed to question that Ole was given the exclusive key to this and other "mysteries." Members were taught that a community was the only place where one could become a real believer and experience the "full counsel of God." Without community, a disciple could never expect to understand the mysteries of God and could never progress very deeply into the Christian life. It was only in community that the individual believer could lose his identity completely in the Bride of Christ, the Church. Ole's interpretation of the passage in John 3:16 where it stated, "God so loved the world that He gave his only begotten Son," is "God so loved the Bride" with the "Bride" being the true church. God only wanted a relationship with His Bride, and only by becoming a part of the Bride could one hope to find salvation.

That was the mystery of life. The true message of God, which Ole had uncovered, was that one must die to self. Only in community — only in a body — could one learn how to die to self. The process of discipleship was the process of purging self-centeredness — any thought of self — and could only be achieved in a community.

CHAPTER 4

✠

Cult of Personality

In Dr. Singer's book, *Cults in Our Midst*, she explained, "In my study of cults, I find that the personality, preferences, and desires of the leader are central in the evolution of any of these groups. Cults are truly personality cults. Because cult structure is basically authoritarian, the personality of the leader is all important." [1] Cults depend on strong charismatic leaders. Without a charismatic type of leadership, cults cannot develop. Charismatic leaders have a strong need for power, enormous levels of self-confidence, and an unshakeable conviction in the correctness of their beliefs.

When a leader has the quality of charisma, he is able to arouse an extraordinary level of trust and devotion from his followers. The charismatic leader attracts people to his ideas and causes them to desire to be in his presence. Charisma can also provide an arena that permits manipulative behavior on the part of the leader and allows him to get away with actions and behavior that most of us would not tolerate from someone without this quality.

It would be difficult to argue that the self-appointed leader of the Trinity Foundation, Ole Anthony, did not possess charisma. At six feet three, he not only had a commanding presence and appearance, but he also exuded a captivating, self-confident air. There was a certainty that encompassed everything he said or did that created a sense of trust in his followers. With his extraordinary rhetorical talent and highly tuned skills of persuasion, Ole possessed the ability to inspire others. Furthermore, with his overpowering conviction that he had been granted special spiritual insights, Ole radiated an intriguing aura. When asked what his first impression of Ole was, one of the members of the Trinity Foundation replied, "Extremely charismatic. Extraordinarily intelligent. I remember women coming up to him and propositioning him. It happened constantly and I was always stunned by it."

Enhancing his ability to draw people in through his strong charismatic personality was the portrait which he painted of himself. Ole often talked of his travels throughout the world, his involvement in politics, his years in the military when he worked as a spy for the Defense Intelligence Agency, and his lavish lifestyle as a millionaire businessman. Even more intoxicating to those who came under his influence, however, was his claim to possess special knowledge of the mysteries of God that he had uncovered in his studies of the Bible and ancient Jewish writings.

With Ole's self-assured manner, few people questioned the veracity of his background. One former member, Michael, recounted his initial impression of Ole:

> Most of us were young, just starting out in our careers, while others of us were still in school. Here was this sophisticated, self-assured man who talked about traveling all around the world, being involved in politics, a former millionaire businessman who had owned his own company and who had given up everything to follow God and start his own Bible study group. We were young; we

were naïve; we believed in him and we wanted nothing more than to be involved with this exciting person. It was many years later that I realized that everything I had believed was a lie. The man who I believed had the key to the mysteries of the kingdom of God and who I thought was the picture of spirituality, constantly and continually misrepresented himself. Even though I left the Trinity Foundation eight years ago, Ole Anthony still remains an enigma. His inordinate need for control, his grandiose version of himself, and his sense of entitlement continue to mystify me.

Ex-proselytes of the Trinity Foundation and other cultic groups often struggle to make sense of the character of the leader. Some continue to carry an image of their guru that is detrimental to the healing process. An understanding of the true nature of the motivation, powers, and abilities of the charismatic leader of spiritually abusive groups is vital to the former member's well-being and spiritual recovery. Although acquiring this understanding can be a speculative venture, there are certain characteristics that all cult leaders have in common.

In his book, *Prophetic Charisma: the Psychology of Revolutionary Religious Personalities*, Len Oakes explores the common personality traits of charismatic leaders, or "prophets," as he labels them. Oakes defines a prophet as someone who promotes a message of salvation that is at odds with traditional beliefs of mainstream Christianity and who has the ability to attract followers who look to him for spiritual guidance and direction in their daily lives. Oakes contends that the core distinctiveness of these individuals is a narcissistic personality disorder, which ultimately develops into the charismatic personality.[2] The primary characteristics of the narcissistic personality disorder are a pattern of grandiosity, an excessive need for admiration, a sense of entitlement, and a lack of empathy for others. Individuals with this personality disorder have an exaggerated sense of their own importance and a constant need for attention. Narcissistic Personality Disorder is a pervasive psychological disorder, which is extremely hard to treat. In contrast to mental illnesses such as major depression, which may be caused by chemical or subtle structural abnormalities in the brain, personality disorders represent a defect or flaw in the person's inner being. It is a fault in the way one's character is developed. Most experts believe that a deep disturbance in the make-up of the individual's personality is indicative of a serious problem in the early developmental years when the basic self was constructed. Although numerous psychological theories have been offered in an attempt to explain the phenomenon of narcissism, essentially all of these theories assert that developmental problems in childhood are the root cause of the formation of the narcissistic personality disorder.

The early months and years of an individual's life are crucial in the development of his personality, and the faulty parenting of dysfunctional families can result in the failure of the child to transition through normal stages of development. In his extensive research of the psychology of religious personalities, Oakes derived his theory that the development of the charismatic personality begins during the early stages of life because of the failure of the young child to grow out of his initial narcissistic view of life. Utilizing one of the major theorists in the twentieth-century's psychoanalytic movement, Heinz Kohut, and his concept of personality formation, Oakes describes how the charismatic leader evolves, stating that in the first few months of life, the child is in a symbiotic, intensively interdependent relationship with his primary love object or "carer."[3] In most cases, the mother is the carer, but as Oakes points out, the role can be played by others in the child's life since it is the child's constructive inner parent, the "self-object" with whom the child has a relationship that is pivotal in the development of adult narcissism. Kohut believes that narcissism is a normal developmental milestone and that the healthy person grows out of his infantile narcissism where he was the center of the universe in his caregiver's eyes. [4]

During the first months of a child's life, he has no awareness of a separation between his self and the external world. In the second stage, generally between two to five months of age, the child becomes psychologically bonded to his main caregiver, usually his mother. During this stage, he is developmentally unable to distinguish between his sense of self and his primary caretaker. He experiences being the center of his mother's world and develops a sense of oneness with her that creates feelings of omnipotence. Narcissism begins in the infant's early attachment to the mother. He consequently perceives her as his powerful life force, whose only function is to cater to his every need, protect him, and adore him. If this initial narcissism extends beyond its usual time, the child's image of the world never changes; therefore, he develops a deepening sense of entitlement and inflated sense of self-importance.

In normal human development, the infant gradually becomes aware of the boundary between himself and his mother. He begins to see that he and his mother are separate beings and the world does not revolve around his every need and desire. The role of the caregiver is to increasingly introduce the realities of the world in such a way that the child is not exposed to dangers or difficult situations that he does not yet have the skills to handle. The mother also takes on the task of interpreting confusing or upsetting events so that the realities of life are understood and integrated into the child's worldview. For the narcissistic child, the mother acts as a filter between the child and the outside world, and protects him in such a way that the child never develops a full understanding of external reality and continues to believe that the world exists for him and him alone.

For individuals with personality disorders, something goes awry during these developmental stages. Some theorists believe that one of the causes of narcissistic personality disorder occurs when the child tries to establish his independence by moving into the differentiation stage while an overprotective mother keeps him in the earlier symbiotic stage by attending to his every need. If the caregiver is overprotective and over-involved with the child, the child does not establish an individual sense of self and identity, but, rather, develops a distorted view of the world and his relation to it. By idealizing the child and protecting him from even the slightest injury, the mother, or caregiver, produces a child with an egocentric view of the world and an inflated sense of himself. An emotionally needy mother may hinder the child's movement from the symbiotic stage, resulting in an exaggerated sense of entitlement and pattern of grandiosity and that continues throughout the individual's life.[5] Interestingly, this is the same sort of "smother love" that Adolf Hitler's mother reportedly exhibited. Because the child has incompletely worked through this fundamental developmental task—separating from his mother—as an adult, he is seen as a sort of *enfant terrible*.

In Ole's case, he had a very young mother who was married to a much older man. While Ole was an infant/toddler, his father was busy traveling and trying to establish a business, and did not appear to focus on the emotional needs of his young wife. However, since she had a new baby boy, it is not hard to imagine that Ole's mother concentrated most of her attention on him.

Little is known of Ole's childhood and early adulthood before he started the Trinity Foundation, except for the few revelations that he presented throughout the years. Most of his background is unverifiable. An inability to validate Ole's background necessitates providing the only accounts which are available from what has been written in newspaper or magazine articles, where he was interviewed by a reporter or from former members' recollections of the details of his life which he had shared with them.

What follows is Ole's own account of his childhood and young adulthood, as well as information since the time that he assumed the leadership of Trinity Foundation. In recounting his background, I have used both information from written sources and from ex-members.

Ole's mother grew up in Montana, the child of a poor Norwegian family. When she was sixteen, she moved to Minnesota to wed a wealthy man more than twice her age in an arranged marriage, which apparently was the custom among Norwegian immigrants at that time. When his mother was barely seventeen, she gave birth to her first child, Ole, on October 3, 1938. Ole described his father as an emotionally distant man who was intensely focused on becoming wealthy. He owned a trucking company in the small Minnesota community where Ole was raised. Unfortunately, the company eventually went bankrupt, which Ole said caused his father much disgrace and humiliation. Unable to stand the shame of bankruptcy, his father moved the family to Arizona, where Ole lived until he turned seventeen. In Arizona, his mother often worked as a nurse, but his father never recovered from the deep humiliation of losing his business. According to Ole, he drank heavily and would often leave his family for weeks at a time. At some point, Ole's parents divorced.

Ole would sometimes talk about his father's continual struggle to regain his self-worth. His father died when Ole was in his thirties, and Ole related his experience when he attended the funeral. During the funeral, Ole described his emotional reaction over his father's death when he broke down and cried, and in his words, "cried for what might have been." Ole described his devastation over the realization that he and his father had never had a real relationship, and when his father died, he realized that it was too late.

It is often said that we derive our image of God from our earthly fathers. If so, Ole's father provided an image of a deity who was distant, wrathful, and unmerciful. Ole shared stories of his father that portrayed a man with little compassion or ability to relate to his son. One story that he told to describe his father was the account of when Ole was a young boy of about five years old and had the whooping cough. Sometimes he would cough so much that he was unable to control his bowels. His father would torture him with ridicule and contempt for soiling his pants and give him a harsh spanking.

Nevertheless, Ole maintained that he had a normal childhood. In William Lobdell's interview with Ole, "Onward Christian Soldier," published in the *Los Angeles Times* on December 8, 2002, the reporter wrote that, according to Ole, "something snapped" when he turned sixteen and he became his hometown's "most notorious juvenile delinquent." One Easter morning he went out to an amphitheater where an Easter sunrise service was to take place and torched a wooden cross. Ole was arrested and given the option of going to jail or enlisting in the military.

Military records validate that Ole was, in fact, in the Air Force, and his listed date of service began on March 13, 1956. While the anecdote regarding his burning of the cross makes an interesting story, this could not have been the precipitating factor to his entry into the military, because the date he entered the service was two weeks prior to the date of Easter. In the year 1956, Easter Sunday was on April 1.

Ole often recalled the story of torching the cross as the causative event for his entry into the military; however, former members also recall another anecdote, which may have been closer to the truth. When Ole was seventeen years of age, he stole drugs from the hospital where his mother worked as a nurse. His mother was horrified when he was accused of this crime and the local law enforcement agreed to not charge him if he would join the military. Whatever the precipitating incident, it is verifiable from military records that Ole was in the Air Force from March 13, 1956 to March 12, 1962—and on active duty from March 13, 1956, to December 10, 1959. Military records indicate that Ole was discharged as an Airman Second Class.

During his time in the Air Force, Ole reported that he was with the Defense Intelligence Agency and traveled all around the world as a surveillance operative monitoring the atomic weapons activities of other countries. In the article entitled, "The Terror of the Televangelists," published by *D Magazine* in its April 1992 issue, Casey Miller wrote:

> Oddly enough, Anthony came upon the religious life after being a spy and a Republican organizer. For eleven years, he worked for the Air Force and the Defense Intelligence Agency, traveling the world undercover to investigate groups trying to develop nuclear weapons. He also witnessed sixteen atomic explosions at various United States government test sites. [6]

In later years, when he became founder and president of the Trinity Foundation, Ole alleged that his important assignment in the Air Force provided experience for him in undercover work, which he later used in his surveillance of televangelists. Verification of this information was not attainable; however, according to one ex-military person, it would have been highly improbable for someone in the Air Force with only the rank of Airman Second Class and a high school diploma to be assigned to the Defense Intelligence Agency. This agency, moreover, was not established until October 1, 1961, which further casts doubts on Ole's claim. Interestingly, it was not until after the Trinity Foundation conducted investigations of the televangelists that newspaper articles appeared in which Ole alleged that he served in the Defense Intelligence Agency. His 1968 campaign brochure, when he ran for state representative, bore no mention of being in the DIA, although it did state that he served in the Air Force.

Ole's tale of his life after the Air Force was equally as impressive as his alleged military experience — and even more remarkable for a man raised in a middle-class family who only had one semester of college. On the matter of his education, there appeared to be a number of inconsistencies with statements he made at different times on the same subject. For example, in his campaign brochure of 1968 he claimed to have had a *formal* education from the University of Arizona and postgraduate work in business and science as well. In an article, "Trinity Foundation Leader Inspires Others, (1/14/89) published in *The Dallas Morning News*, reporter Jeffrey Weiss indicated that Ole received his "undergraduate training in geophysics"; however, in another newspaper article, "The Undercover Thorn in Robert Tilton's Side," in the Fort Worth Star-Telegram written three years later (1/26/92), reporter Jim Jones writes that Ole was a pre-med student at Arizona State University." Yet, at other times, Ole admitted that he had never graduated from college.

In an attempt to determine his educational background, multiple calls to universities in Arizona and Colorado were made. According to Arizona State University and several other colleges, there was no record of Ole's enrollment or attendance at these schools. The University of Arizona had records of his attendance there in the fall of 1960. Although he enrolled in the spring semester, university records indicated that he withdrew on February 28, 1961.

Following his discharge from the Air Force, Ole said that he went to work for Teledyne, Incorporated and accumulated a "three-and-one-half-million-dollar Wall Street fortune" that he later lost when his company, Ocean Resources, Incorporated, filed for bankruptcy in 1971 (*Fort Worth Weekly*, "Pounding the Pious," May 8–15, 1997 by Stacy Schnellenbach-Boogel). Ole alleged that he lost this oceanography firm, which specialized in offshore oil exploration when the Santa Barbara oil spill resulted in the secretary of the interior temporarily banning offshore drilling in 1971. Although Ole claimed to have amassed over a three-million-dollar fortune, court records indicated that from 1968 until 1971 numerous lawsuits were filed against him by creditors resulting in financial judgments levied against him.

Much of Ole's well-crafted account of his background was mingled with hyperbole, if not fabrication. There was always enough of the truth that the other details were not questioned. For example, he often talked about the period of his life when he was involved in politics. Ole claimed to have been a Texas Coordinator for the Goldwater-for-President Campaign in 1964. In an interview with Ole, a writer for *D Magazine* said in April 1992, "After retiring from the spy business in the mid-1960s, he (Ole) ... was a Texas coordinator for Goldwater for President '64."[7]

Ole also indicated that in 1966 he was the late Senator John Tower's regional campaign manager, according to the article by Delia M. Rios, "Ole Anthony's Religious Community Lives by an Ancient Code," published in *The Dallas Morning News* on December 22, 1991.

In my research of hundreds of newspaper articles, books, and Internet searches from that time period in the 1960s regarding those two campaigns, I was unable to find one reference to Ole in either one of these two campaigns. I did uncover a copy of Ole's campaign brochure when he ran in the 1968 race for a seat in the Texas House of Representatives. Interestingly, this publicity material, which was printed in 1968, made no mention of Ole's role as a Goldwater Texas coordinator in 1964 or as regional campaign manager for Tower in 1966. This alleged part of his political career did not surface in any newspaper or magazine article until the late 1980s and 1990s. It seems curious that a political candidate would not mention those significant accomplishments, which supposedly occurred only two to four years prior to his candidacy, among his credentials in his campaign brochure. What was listed in his pamphlet is that he served as precinct chairman, president of the Garland Republican Men's Club, and as a member of the Dallas Grand Ole Party (GOP) Executive committee. While those positions are somewhat impressive, it would seem that serving as a Texas coordinator in the Goldwater presidential campaign and as regional manager in Tower's senate race would be much more prestigious and, thus, worth mentioning in one's campaign brochure.

Another discrepancy between Ole's account of his background and the actual historical fact is the claim, which he made in both public conversations and in several newspaper interviews published from the 1990s to the present, that he had been one of the Dallas delegates to the National Republican Convention in 1968. One of several articles in which Ole reported that he had been a delegate to the convention was in an interview Brad Bailey published in the *Dallas Observer* on July 18, 1991. In Bailey's article, "The Guru of East Dallas," he wrote that in that same year (1968), he was a delegate to the Republican National Convention and ran as an at-large candidate for the Texas State Legislature, losing by only a few thousand votes, he (Ole) says." However, another article, "Chance Encounter Has Chain Reaction," published in *The Dallas Morning News* during that time (August 17, 1968) described an interaction that Ole had with the Reverend Ralph Abernathy at the Republican National Convention. Abernathy had been seated next to Ole and apparently had used Ole's name when he told television reporters that he wanted to address the national convention and was planning to do so with the aid of Ole Anthony. In the newspaper article, the reporter wrote:

> Just how did Anthony, who wasn't even a delegate to the convention, end up on network television sitting next to the chairman of the Southern Leadership Conference? Anthony gave this account: As a state representative candidate for Place 3 in Dallas County, Anthony was given the title of honorary sergeant-at-arms at the convention. "I was just sitting there in my seat, and noticed a big rash of movement coming in. They (50 members of the Poor People's March) came up to the aisle to me, and suddenly there was Abernathy sitting next to me. We were both in our assigned seats." [8]

It appears that although Ole claimed through numerous newspaper articles that he had been a delegate to the 1968 Republican Convention, the actual truth was that he had been given the title of honorary sergeant-at-arms because he was a state representative candidate. Of all the claims that Ole made concerning his "political career," the only verifiable claim was that he was a candidate in the 1968 race for a seat in the Texas House of Representatives, but was not elected.

If these dubious statements had been made before Ole had founded the Trinity Foundation and made a career out of exposing the hypocrisies of the televangelists, one might be able to dismiss the inconsistencies concerning his own background as being of little importance; however, for an individual who preached that men of God should adhere to rigid honesty and be highly accountable, it is troubling that there are so many discrepancies regarding his background and his life.

By Ole's own account, he enlisted in the Air Force at age seventeen, spent eleven years carrying out surveillance missions for the Defense Intelligence Agency by monitoring Chinese and Soviet nuclear weapons programs; observed the explosion of the hydrogen bomb in the South Pacific; witnessed dozens of nuclear tests; became the Texas Coordinator for the Goldwater-for-President campaign; was regional campaign manager for John Tower; ran for state legislature; accrued a Wall Street fortune of three and one-half million dollars while working at Teledyne; and founded his own oceanography company—all before the age of thirty-three! Amazing accomplishments for a young man with only a high school education and one semester of college.

After his company failed in 1971, Ole said he served as finance campaign manager for Wes Wise's mayoral candidacy and served as director of Dallas's War on Poverty. During this period, he was also said to have started a public relations firm with Wes Wise, former mayor of Dallas. His public relations firm was hired to launch a Dallas Christian television station and he later became a religious broadcaster for the station, hosting television talk shows and then, later, radio talk shows. In relating his experience, Ole would say that he was appalled by the inferiority of Christian media and became disillusioned when he witnessed preachers transformed into merchants, whose purpose was to use the airwaves to generate money for their ministries. Around 1971 to 1972, Ole is said to have experienced a religious conversion and it was shortly after this experience that he founded the Trinity Foundation, Incorporated, along with two other men.

According to public records, articles of incorporation for Trinity Foundation were filed with the state of Texas, and the foundation was formally chartered as a non-profit organization on January 31, 1973. Trinity Foundation's early mission was for the production of Christian media. Around 1974, the organization promoted an outdoor concert featuring Pat Boone and Andre Crouch and the Disciples, which was rained out, and once again, Ole found himself at the helm of a bankrupt enterprise. Years later, Ole would say that this failure was an act of God. Christians in the media were focused on prosperity and equated success with God's blessing. Ole came to view their perspective as utter blasphemy.

During the early years of the Trinity Foundation, Ole hosted religious talk shows, while preaching the virtues of an austere lifestyle and teaching a Bible study to a small gathering of friends and acquaintances. These media activities brought Ole little income, so his primary means of support was from the few people who were attending his Bible study group. A married couple that started attending the group in 1975 recalled that Ole was the only employee of the Trinity Foundation at that time. Barry and Janice were not members of any church, so they gave a tenth of their income to the Trinity Foundation. Their tithes helped pay for the rent at the office and provided money for Ole's living expenses. At that time, he hosted a radio talk show and worked out an arrangement with one of the advertisers. In exchange for commercials, the advertiser gave him credit for meals at a restaurant in Dallas. Ole was living in the Trinity Foundation's one-room office, and when he did not eat at the restaurant he was always welcome to eat at one of his group members' homes.

During his media days, he also hosted a television talk show. The format of the program consisted of interviews with such people as Corrie Ten Boom and Billy Graham. Ole had the series of interviews compiled for a book titled *Cross Fire*, and one of his first conflicts with a televangelist occurred when he was promoting the book. He was asked to be a part of Jim and Tammy Faye Bakker's television program, and Ole related his version of the experience:

> We went to this garish, white-trash set, with big flow-
> ers and big hair, and the lights were on, and we were
> about to start the interview, when Jim pulled the plug,
> Anthony says, claiming the values of poverty and humil-
> ity in the book's prologue upset Bakker so much that he
> canceled the segment. [9]

Although Ole purportedly had led a lavish lifestyle prior to 1973, he was now embracing an ascetic way of life. His earned income reported to the Internal Revenue Services from 1974 to 1981 averaged less than two thousand dollars a year. Around 1977, Ole's radio-hosting days ended, and, for a while, the only thing going on was the Bible study/ fellowship group that Trinity Foundation sponsored. The group grew and evolved into what Ole called the *body*—a group of believers who were committed to one another and to their charismatic leader.

Ole was the only employee of the foundation until the early 1980s when the concept of the Levites was introduced and the foundation had other paid employees. Ole and the other Levites were paid a salary of eighty dollars a week and provided shelter consisting of a single room or shared apart-ment. Out of their meager salary, Levites paid thirty dollars a week toward their meals at the Lair and, of course, were expected to tithe. Because the foundation did not receive outside funding, it depended solely on the tithes and offerings of its members and, therefore, giving was a major emphasis. All members were expected to tithe—that is, give one-tenth of their gross income to the foundation.

Additionally, once a year there was an accounting of one's income and expenses called First Fruits meetings. The concept of First Fruits was derived from the Old Testament days when the people brought an offering of the first crops of their harvest. For Trinity Foundation this was an annual event, which required a full disclosure of one's revenue from the previous year, current assets, and an accounting of how one spent his money. These meetings were attended by the member, his or her Bible study teacher(s), and of course, Ole. The member submitted a worksheet detailing his income and expenses, which was then reviewed by Ole, and an annual first fruit tithe was assessed—generally, one week's salary. These meetings were voluntary; however, we were reminded of the story of Ananias and his wife, Sapphira, a couple in the Bible who kept back part of their assets, while others in the New Testament Church were giving sacrificially. Ananias and Sapphira died as punishment for lying about giving all their proceeds to the church.

Another source of revenue for Trinity Foundation was the asset tithe, which was a once-in-a-lifetime offering assessed utilizing information from one's annual income and the gross value of all assets. During the assessment process, the member's detailed list of all his/her assets, list of current debt, as well as the amount tithed in the previous year were reviewed. Utilizing that data, an asset tithe was levied. The asset tithe was not mandatory, but was done as an act symbolizing a member's desire to permanently join the community, when the member realized that he was "home."

Although there were a number of individuals and families who were comfortably affluent, there was also a large group of members for whom money was a constant struggle. Bible study groups were often called on to assist any of the Levites or other members in their group when additional financial needs arose.

Ole, however, never seemed to have any financial needs. Around 1979 Ole was injured at a health spa where he was a member. According to court documents, Ole was sitting on a bench in the inhalation room when his left foot came in contact with an electrical outlet that had exposed wires, which resulted in an electrical shock. The lawsuit filed by Ole's attorney requested damages in the amount of at least $789,452.69 and the case was settled sometime in the 1980s. The exact amount of the settlement is unknown, as is what became of the money. Former members had huge variations, from $30,000 to $300,000 in the amounts that they said Ole told them he had received. Several of them also remembered that Ole confessed at some point years later that he had not tithed on the settlement and decided to do so. Ex-members also remembered such things as his having an account with Merrill Lynch and that he always did his own taxes. Many also recalled that he would go weeks and sometimes months without cashing his weekly paycheck from Trinity Foundation.

Although Ole appeared to have no need for money, during the years I was a member he had a girlfriend who had constant financial needs. Shortly after I became a member in 1993, Ole began dating Suzette. Suzette had numerous physical ailments and eventually felt that she could no longer work in the outside world, so she became a Levite. Unlike the other Levites who did bona fide work for the foundation, Suzette's main job appeared to be that of planting and watering flowers and other plants. Her first Trinity-funded living arrangement was with Amanda and Jake. While remodeling one of the houses on the block, which they had purchased, Amanda and Jake were asked if they would convert one of the rooms into a bedroom and bath, with a private entrance for Suzette. She lived there a year or so before she and Amanda had a falling out. Suzette then moved into a small apartment on the block, which was painted and fixed up by the Levites, until the owner requested that Suzette move out. She then relocated to one of the condominiums, and again had the Levites refurbish it until it reached her standard. Although the other unmarried Levites lived in austere settings in single rooms in the Lair House, the Trinity office, or shared an apartment together, Suzette had her own place, which caused some controversy. When she moved into the condominium, it was with the understanding that she would get a job and pay the expenses herself. However, when I left Trinity Foundation she had been in the condominium over six months and still had not gone back to work. Suzette's situation was another of the issues at Trinity Foundation, which was not discussed openly; however, there was an undercurrent of resentment throughout most of the community.

As Amanda said, "It wasn't the fact that she got preferential treatment from Ole, she was his girlfriend and that was normal. My issues with Suzette were always regarding how she was treated at the foundation. She was always given power—and never had to participate in any of the chores that the rest of us were expected to do. She rarely washed dishes or served meals at the Lair, never helped with the children, and never helped set up for Seder. She was there to be served and she got away with it. I certainly talked privately about it to Ole. And the answer was always, 'She's not treated special. No one else has problems with this.' He always tried to allude to the fact that I was jealous of Suzette because she was his girlfriend. My issue was that I paid tithes to the foundation to help people, not to be Suzette's sugar daddy."

Another concern that a former member expressed was that although Ole had no formal training in theology, he gave the impression that he was a superior self-taught theologian. He often claimed to have several volumes of notes that he had taken from the twelve years which he spent translating the Bible and studying the *Old Testament*, the *Torah*, the *Talmud*, the *Zohar*, and other ancient religious writings.

Most Christian denominations require seminary training before an individual can be ordained or licensed to serve as clergy. A sound theological education provides a foundation for rightly interpreting scripture. Without a solid theological background, it is too easy for a zealous believer to be caught up in some tangent or another. Our society requires practitioners to be licensed for public welfare and safety. Licensing provides the assurance that the individual has completed a minimal level of competency and is qualified to practice in his discipline. Just as our society requires professionals such as physicians, counselors, dentists, plumbers, etc., to have a license to ensure that they have undertaken the necessary study and training to be qualified in their professions, is it not even more imperative that ministers be qualified since they occupy an unparalleled position of trust and authority?

Although Ole preached against "lone rangers" in the Christian faith, he did, in fact, fit the profile of a lone ranger. Trinity Foundation was not a part of a denomination, nor was Ole ordained as a minister. He never received formal theological training, nor did he surround himself with other theologians. Ole was not vested with any legitimate authority by any recognized denomination. His only authority was that which he arrogated to himself.

One of Ole's favorite sayings was, "If it isn't two thousand years old, it's crap." In fact, the whole enterprise that Ole embarked upon in trying to recreate the experience of the first century Christians was quixotic, as any genuine scholar of the New Testament and its historical background could tell you. In his landmark study of Christian origins, *The New Testament and the People of God*, theologian N. T. Wright discussed this type of thinking:

> If early Christianity is to function in any way as a norm, the process will clearly involve selection ... of types of early Christianity according to a pre-arranged *evaluative* scheme ... There are more types of early Christianity than can be easily grouped together and given authoritative status. And on this point — since on the model being

used the norm is of no significance — one is forced to import other criteria from the inside, which will enable us to distinguish the 'right' sort of early religious experience from the 'wrong' source. Either one must elevate the earliest period on the grounds of its being primitive and therefore purer; or one will take a particular *type* of religion, described according to either its cultural provenance (Jewish or Greek) or its conformity to a theological norm (Pauline Christianity, for instance). And this again seems highly problematic: where did these criteria come from? They do not seem to have come from the Bible or tradition. They can only have come from the interpreter's view of what mainstream, or 'authentic' early Christianity was really like. [10]

In C. FitzSimons Allison's book, *The Cruelty of Heresy*, he states:

> Unless guided by the Church's creeds and Councils, I believe I would produce the most virulent heretical distortions of scriptures. This recognition stems from a humility, however inadequate, that I would be delighted to share with those whose confidence in themselves leads them to devalue the creeds and Councils. [11]

In focusing on the first-century church and its understanding of Christianity and denying the work of the Holy Spirit in the church's history, Ole ignored the profound achievements of the Christian church in the fourth and fifth centuries in the development of guidelines for Christian orthodoxy. The Councils were initiated in response to sincere individuals and leaders, like Ole, who were teaching heresy. Jesus said that He would send the Holy Spirit to guide believers into all truth. God has been at work in the church throughout the course of its history, and to devalue what the church has learned in the last two thousand years is to devalue the work of the Holy Spirit.

A sound theological education provides an arena where there is accountability that encourages academic and theological integrity. Had Ole received theological training from an accredited school, perhaps he would not have developed his own private doctrine. Without an understanding of hermeneutics, which is the science of the principles and methods for interpretation of the Bible, Ole created his own doctrine, which was infused with allegorical interpretations. His doctrinal teachings did not coincide with the orthodox teaching and methods of interpreting the Bible. Orthodoxy—that is, right doctrine—has been established over a period of two thousand years by Christian leaders and theologians who have struggled with the complexity of doctrinal truth. Ole did not see the Bible as the only authoritative source, but relied on other manuscripts and books with symbolic, allegorical, and mystic elements to establish his theology. In fact, Ole ridiculed the mainstream Christian belief that insists that the Bible is the only true authoritative source of knowledge by insisting that this was a form of idolatry. "The Bible is not the Word of God. It's words written about the Word of God, who is Jesus." Christians who reverenced scripture were accused of worshiping a book. One time to illustrate his point, Ole set a Bible on fire.

Ole used his sources eclectically and uncritically in order to promote his own doctrinal teaching. Some of the books that he read and studied, such as the *Zohar*, are considered occult-like by mainstream theologians. The *Zohar* is based on the writings of second-century scholar Simeon bar Yochai, and Ole believed that this highly advanced treatise could help him decipher the hidden meanings embedded in the arrangement of letters and words in the *Torah*. The *Zohar* is full of fantastical descriptions of angels, chariots, ancient alphabets, golems (monsters) and biblical figures, and Ole used much of what he studied in these writings in his Bible studies. It made for very interesting Bible studies since these were concepts to which most members had never been exposed.

Ole would often ridicule anyone with a religious background or anyone who had theological training. He would say things like, "I don't care about your silly schools of thought derived by man. I'm about the real truth." In many ways, Ole's theology was filled with Gnostic tendencies. Gnosticism is characterized by claims to have special knowledge apart from the authority of scripture. Ole often said that at the point he became a believer, he had been given all knowledge and understanding and that he never learned anything that he did not know on that spectacular day. The Gnostic believes that God dwells in every man and that real spiritual birth starts when there is an awareness of the indwelling of the divine spirit. Once the "spirit of God" is perceived, the full knowledge of God is attained and spiritual maturity is achieved.

The term *cult* can generally be used to describe a religious group that centers on an individual or group of individuals who claim to have received a special revelation from God. The individual will claim that his teaching has always been the truth, but that somehow the church abandoned the true revelation of God. A cult leader considers himself superior to the church and its schools. The cult leader believes he has received a special understanding of scripture. Over time, his opinion of himself becomes inflated, and if the number of followers increases, it provides a growing sense of power and affirmation that he truly is God's spokesman.

In *The Guru Papers: Masks of Authoritarian Power*, the authors, Joel Kramer and Diana Alstad, define cults as groups that have an authoritarian structure where:

> ... the leader's power is not constrained by scripture, tradition, or any other "higher" authority ... In a cult, absolute authority lies in a leader who has few if any external constraints. This means the leader (who is

usually the founder) is not merely the interpreter but is also the creator of truth, and thus has free rein in what he proposes. Whether or not his authority rests upon a tradition or religion, he is revered as either God's unique vessel or as an actual manifestation of the living God or the god-force. [12]

It appears that with the growth of the membership of the Trinity Foundation, Ole felt that his role was similar to that of the apostle Paul. One former member recalled that when Ole returned from a trip to Greece, he seemed to have actually envisioned himself as the apostle Paul. He began talking about creating a one-man show where he would portray the apostle Paul and people would then ask questions of him.

Another alarming clue that his perception of his own importance may have been increasing surfaced when he returned from a trip to Austria where he had seen the Lance of Longinus in a museum. The Lance of Longinus supposedly was the spear that pierced the side of Christ during His crucifixion. Its name was derived from the owner, Longinus, and because it had pierced the side of Christ, it was thought to contain incredible powers. A legend grew around the lance that whoever possessed it would be able to conquer the world. According to the legend, Napoleon attempted to obtain the weapon after the battle of Austerlitz and Charlemagne actually carried the lance in forty-seven successful battles, but died when he accidentally dropped it. The spear eventually came into the possession of the House of the Habsburgs and, by 1912, it was on exhibit at the Hofburg Museum in Austria.

When Ole returned from his trip to Austria, he told his followers that he had seen the Lance of Longinus and, in an incredible epiphany, he had taken possession spiritually of the spear. His account was strangely like the account of Hitler's described in Trevor Ravenscroft's book, *The Spear of Destiny*. According to Ravenscroft, in September of 1912, a young

Adolf Hitler, learning of the lance and its reputation, visited the museum. Dr. Walter Stein, who accompanied Hitler on that visit, remembered:

> When we first stood side by side in front of the Spear of Destiny it appeared to me that Hitler was in so deep a condition of trance that he was suffering almost complete sense-denudation and a total lack of self-consciousness. Hitler later said, "I stood there quietly gazing upon it for several minutes quite oblivious to the scene around me. It seemed to carry some hidden inner meaning which evaded me, a meaning which I felt I inwardly knew yet could not bring to consciousness … I felt as though I myself had held it before in some earlier century of history. That I myself had once claimed it as my talisman of power and held the destiny of the world in my hands …".[13]

Did Ole really believe that he had spiritual possession of the spear? If so, what were the implications of such a grandiose statement? Ole claimed to have all knowledge. He understood all spiritual truth and members testified to his incredible spiritual insights. One former member provided this observation into the inner nature of Ole:

> Ole saw the world in terms of flesh and spirit. I think Ole did have a particular type of insight, although I am not sure that "insight" is the right word. He had the same type of insight that an accomplished con man has. His insight had much to do with what people's "buttons" were and how to manipulate them. For example, Ole was an extraordinary card-player. He could sit down at a table, size up his opponents quickly, and win most of the hands. Rather than being about luck or intellect, poker is a psychological contest of wills. Winning in poker has more to do with an ability to see when other people are lying and when other people are genuinely confident and not just lying about it. Over time, if you are a good reader

of people, as Ole is, you will win because the whole game has to do with bluffing. I believe that was Ole's particular and remarkable talent — to read people with incredible astuteness and speed, and to know how to manipulate them. In some context, you could say that this was seeing in the spirit, but Ole *was* good at a level that went beyond just having good observation skills. His ability was more of an intuitive thing.

Former members recalled that numerous times during the early years of Trinity Foundation, Ole would threaten to leave. One particular incident stood out in Moira's memory:

> Ole got angry with us for some reason and told us that we were like brute beasts that were too stupid to understand the things of God and he was quitting. He was not going to continue the Bible studies. With that proclamation, he got up and went to his bedroom. At that time, Ole was living in the home of one member's grandmother who had recently died. While the estate was being settled, Ole had been allowed to live there at no cost. The Bible studies were also being held in this home; and so on this occasion when Ole threatened to quit as our leader, he went to his bedroom and locked the door. One of the members, Paul, went to the door of the bedroom and started knocking on it, begging Ole not to quit. When Ole refused to open the door, Paul sat down outside his door and cried, imploring Ole not to leave us, promising him that we would try harder. The rest of us sat around wondering what to do next and finally left, but Paul continued to cry outside of his door. Ole's threatening to quit became a common occurrence and we always promised to try harder. Ole always came back because God told him to do so. In later years, he would remind us that he never wanted to be our leader, but God constrained him, and he had no choice but to obey God.

Ole once said, "If you have a preacher who can't answer all your questions, fire him. My job is to have the answers for you." The accolades he received from his followers must have been very intoxicating for this man who had failed at everything — politics, business, relationships. Now he had a group of people who sat at his feet and acknowledged that he had the answers to life.

Had he not been so persuasive in his claim to have special knowledge, along with his aura of spirituality that was captivating and passionate, had he not been such a charming and accomplished seducer who added to his own mystique by embellishing on his past, would we still have succumbed to his charisma? Would we have gotten caught up in his teachings and his way of life?

Max Weber, one of the founders of sociology, defined charisma as "a certain quality of an individual personality by virtue of which he is considered extraordinary and treated as endowed with supernatural, superhuman, or at least specifically exceptional powers ... [that] are regarded as of divine origin." Weber goes on to say that the leader's disciples are as much a source of his power as are his unique skills, for without his followers, he is nothing. [14] Ole would say that he was at perfect peace. He claimed for himself emotional and spiritual perfection. He was beyond having any types of those human frailties that everyone else had. He maintained that he never once considered what he was going to say, he was only led by the Spirit. Ole clearly saw himself as the anointed who had a special relationship with the Father. Just as Christ's disciple, Peter, said to Jesus, "To whom shall we go? You have the words of life," Ole's disciples came to believe that he alone had the keys to the kingdom of God.

CHAPTER 5

✝

We Can Walk on Fire

One of the primary doctrines that Ole taught was that an individual's mind was the "antichrist." The antichrist was not some being that would appear on earth during the latter days, the antichrist was you. Your mind was always against Christ, was always in opposition to God, and therefore, could not be trusted. To support his doctrine, Ole used a verse from Isaiah, "For my thoughts are not your thoughts, neither are your ways my ways, saith the Lord (Isaiah 55:8), as well as Jeremiah 17:9, "The heart is deceitful above all things, and desperately wicked: who can know it?"

Because we cannot see things from God's perspective and because our hearts are pure evil, we cannot trust ourselves. Ole would frequently make statements, such as, "Don't judge after the senses. See past the appearance. See in the spirit." In Ole's theology, an individual could not trust his senses because what he thought was good might not be, and what he thought was bad might not be. The confusion that arises when you are constantly told that your mind is the enemy is massive. Your capacity to think is undermined.

In many ways, Ole had discovered the perfect mind control doctrine. Ole continually exhorted his followers "to go to war with your minds" and in doing so, he corroded their self-trust. Ultimately, this had the effect of changing Ole's disciples' perception of reality, and they became increasingly dependent on this leader who claimed that he could see in the spirit. If you can persuade people to believe that their own minds are the enemy, then you have them absolutely in your power. Individuals who are unable to trust themselves become susceptible to the manipulation of the "enlightened" leader.

An example of where this mindset can lead can be seen in one of the most bizarre episodes in the history of the Trinity Foundation—the fire-walking event. The practice of fire-walking has existed for thousands of years in dozens of different cultures and refers to walking over hot coals, rocks, or cinders. Done properly, it is possible to accomplish this without burning the soles of your feet. The Trinity fire-walking event, however, was probably one of Ole's most embarrassing moments.

The group, as they often did, traveled out to a ranch owned by one member's family for a weekend retreat. The first evening Ole began to prepare his disciples to walk on hot coals by introducing the subject and explaining his purpose for this demonstration. Ole explained to his minions that their faith was shallow and weak because it had never been tested. The individual's mind tells him things, but it is a false perception—not reality. This experience was to be a powerful tool to free the followers from the constricting shackles of their natural way of thinking. Ole reminded his disciples that the normal way we think is calculating without God, seeing without faith; however, God desires that the believer move through life always seeing that with God, all things are possible.

Through the fire-walking experience, Ole would demonstrate that the mind could not be trusted. The mind was always lying and would particularly do so in this arena by convincing us that our feet would be burned if we walked on the coals. However, by overcoming the fear of walking on hot coals, we would truly understand that the mind was the greatest enemy—the antichrist—and thus, prevented the comprehension of the full mysteries of God.

Ole confidently assured everyone that the fire-walking was simply a metaphor for what the unreliable psyche perceived as being unachievable. Once the disciples were able to walk on hot coals without burning their feet, they would better understand how their own minds continually betray them. Furthermore, it would prepare the members for all the potential symbolic fires that they would continue to face in their war against the mind and its lies. It was also a way of ultimately testing who among the believers sincerely wanted to be a part of the mysteries of God. To prepare for this glorious event, Ole had everyone keep a fast from both food and any form of liquids.

Rather than requiring a faith that God can do the impossible and that we are not bound to "cause and effect," the ability to walk on fire actually required faith that we could move fast enough to avoid getting burned. It also required faith that the coals have been prepared properly, which was not done in this case. Instead of spreading a single layer of coals, Dick placed ten bags of charcoal briquettes side by side and simply tore off the top side of the bag. Then, the charcoal was drenched with lighter fluid and the bags were set on fire. After the coals had burned for a couple of hours forming a bed of glowing embers three to four inches deep, the fire-walking event began.

Several people, including Ole, walked across the coals. It soon became clear that the experiment was not working out the way he had planned, and that people were getting burned. Ole, to his credit, cut the event short and had one of the members hose down the coals. Then, everyone went back to the ranch house to process what had just happened.

One of the reasons it is possible for people to walk on hot coals, we later learned, is that the body rapidly sends moisture to the bottoms of the feet when they encounter something like the burning coals. However, since the members had been fasting that day they were all somewhat dehydrated, and this mechanism was not working as well as it might have otherwise. Also, of course, the depth of the fire-bed was such that more of the bottoms of people's feet were touching the coals, which was not supposed to happen.

One former member, Dave, recalled that people cried afterwards, "not so much because people had been hurt, but because our lack of understanding and faith had prevented us from being able to accomplish this test. Many things were said after that to justify the failed experiment, such as the coals were too hot or there are some things in this world we are just not going to get past because of the limitations of being human."

Moira, who was present at the event, recalled the experience: "It really freaked me out that we could blindly follow Ole in that way—without even questioning him. That was really the beginning for me—the beginning of the end. I began thinking again as an individual. The whole situation shocked me and made me realize that if it had been poisonous Kool-Aid instead of hot coals that Ole was using to teach us that our minds lie to us, we would have all drunk the poisonous Kool-Aid and died. It was very scary."

Later that evening, Ole announced that his feet had been seriously injured and he would need to go to the hospital, so Doug, Kay, and another member took him to an emergency room. Ole's explanation to the medical staff was that he had fallen into a campfire. His feet were so severely burned and blistered that he spent the next several weeks in a wheelchair.

CHAPTER 6

Breaking Spirits

"Do you remember the 'hot seats'?" I asked Mark, one of the former members. "Vividly," he replied, "I remember every one of them." Mark was the first ex-member whom I interviewed while I was researching this book. As I was to discover, Mark was not typical of the former members.

Some refused to talk about their experience on the hot seats. "It's too painful. I don't want to relive it, Wendy. I'm sorry. I want to help you but I just can't," I was told over and over. Others simply could not remember or had buried the memories so deeply into the shadowy recesses of their mind that they were no longer retrievable.

I was not yet a member of Trinity Foundation when the hot seats were introduced by Ole. I had heard about them, but not in any detail. I began to understand the intensity and damage done to the members who had been involved in the hot seats after my husband and I left the group and were seeing a counselor. During one counseling session, Doug tried to describe the hot seats to our therapist. In response to Doug's admittedly constrained description, our therapist said, "It sounds like psychological torture—what they did to prisoners of war." Her words haunted me. I thought about one of Doug's closest friends, another former member, who had told us that even today, ten years after leaving Trinity Foundation, he could not see a cross without wanting to destroy it.

Robert Lifton, a psychiatrist and distinguished professor at the City University of New York, wrote the definitive book on the psychology of extremism following his study of the effects of mind control on American prisoners of war under the Communist Chinese during the Korean War. In the following excerpt from *Thought Reform and the Psychology of Totalism: A Study of 'Brainwashing' in China*, Lifton described an aspect of the thought reform process—group confession—which depicted Trinity's hot seats with remarkable clarity:

> Confession is carried beyond its ordinary religious, legal, and therapeutic expressions to the point of becoming a cult in itself. There is the demand that one confess to crimes one has not committed, to sinfulness that is artificially induced, in the name of a cure that is arbitrarily imposed. Such demands are made possible not only by the ubiquitous human tendencies toward guilt and shame but also by the need to give expression to these tendencies. In totalist hands, confession becomes a means of exploiting, rather than offering solace for, these vulnerabilities.
>
> The totalist confession takes on a number of special meanings. It is first a vehicle for the kind of personal purification which we have just discussed, a means of maintaining a perpetual inner emptying or psychological purge of impurity; this purging milieu enhances the totalists' hold upon existential guilt. Second, it is an act of symbolic self-surrender, the expression of the merging of individual and environment. Third, it is a means of maintaining an ethos of total exposure—a policy of making public (or at least known to the Organization)

everything possible about the life experiences, thoughts, and passions of each individual, and especially those elements which might be regarded as derogatory.

The assumption underlying total exposure … is the environment's claim to total ownership of each individual self within it. Private ownership of the mind and its products—of imagination or of memory—becomes highly immoral. The accompanying rationale (or rationalization) is familiar, the milieu has attained such a perfect state of enlightenment that any individual retention of ideas or emotions has become anachronistic.

The cult of confession can offer the individual person meaningful psychological satisfactions in the continuing opportunity for emotional catharsis and for relief of suppressed guilt feelings, especially insofar as these are associated with self-punitive tendencies to get pleasure from personal degradation. More than this, the sharing of confession enthusiasms can create an orgiastic sense of "oneness," of the most intense intimacy with fellow confessors and of the dissolution of self into the great flow of the Movement. And there is also, at least initially, the possibility of genuine self-revelation and of self-betterment through the recognition that "the thing that has been exposed is what I am."

But as totalist pressures turn confession into recurrent command performances, the element of histrionic public display takes precedence over genuine inner experience …. In this sense, the cult of confession has effects quite the reverse of its ideal of total exposure: rather than eliminating personal secrets, it increases and intensifies them …" [1]

In some respects, asking the former members of Trinity Foundation to recall their hot seats was analogous to asking victims of sexual assault to describe what it was like being raped. I had not understood why a rape victim could not recount what happened during a rape or remember the face of their perpetrator. Now I understand that an intense traumatic experience—like that suffered in a rape or a hot seat—often causes emotional amnesia of the event.

As one former member, Dave, stated, "It is difficult to recount the experience I had on the hot seat because I think part of my mind is blanked on most of it. The hot seats felt like a spiritual rape and it isn't something that you want to think about. As a matter of fact, those of us who experienced the hot seats go out of our way not to think about it, because the fear was so massive."

It was easier for people to describe others' hot seats, but even that was limited because of the deep-seated fear that they would somehow be betraying Ole. Again, this is analogous to a sexual assault where the predator convinces his victim that serious harm will come if she ever tells anyone.

In the early years of Trinity Foundation, the primary method of indoctrination was through Ole's teachings and the Bible studies. According to Barry and Janice, two of the original members who met Ole at Christ for the Nations, a Bible institute located in Dallas, there were only about six people attending the weekly Bible study back in 1975 when the group started.

Barry said, "To call it a Bible study would be an overstatement. We never opened our Bibles. We just listened to Ole, but he was extremely charismatic, extraordinarily intelligent, and very interesting.

"We were young—in our early twenties—and had just moved to Dallas. We didn't know anyone and hadn't gotten involved in a church. Ole invited us to his Bible study, so we went. Janice and I attended two years before we finally woke up to the fact that what he was teaching was his own doctrine.

"I was brought up in the Mennonite Brethren denomination, and my parents were missionaries. I knew the Bible, but we still got caught up in Ole's charisma for a while. We considered him our friend. For most of the two years we attended, I was the only one who had a steady job, so our offerings and tithes were primarily what were supporting Ole during that time period."

By the time Barry and Janice left in 1977, the group had grown to about twenty people and they were all becoming close friends. By the early '80s, the Bible studies had expanded to two nights during the week, Sunday morning, and a time of socializing together on Sunday afternoon. Ole, however, must have felt that his Bible studies were not producing the real changes he longed to see in the lives and hearts of his followers.

Dave stated it this way, "You can have people come to Bible study three times a week but that really isn't enough to thoroughly indoctrinate people to the extent that Ole wanted. He needed some other way to profoundly and permanently alter people's personalities and, from his perspective, to fix them. Ole discovered the ultimate method of transformation when he started the hot seats."

In the spring of 1985, Trinity Foundation members embarked on the first of what would be dozens of rounds of psycho-torture sessions known as the hot seats. The "hot seat era" lasted through the early 1990s, and during that period, the hot seats became a daily part of life for the members. The group would go away for long weekends and have marathon sessions. People would curse and scream and cry—eventually arriving at the "orgiastic sense of oneness" described by Lifton.

"For the time is come that judgment must begin at the house of God ..." (1 Peter 4:17) was the proof text from the Bible that Ole used to convince group members that the hot seats were absolutely essential if they were to go into a deeper level of the faith. He taught that in order to avoid total damnation in the afterlife, one must experience the judgment seat here, in this life. You must experientially know that you truly deserve damnation so that at the time of the real judgment seat you will understand that your only hope is to plead for mercy.

Although all of the hot seats had the theme of exposing a member's false worship, the hot seats invariably resulted in focusing on each individual's "shame issues." According to Ole, shame was what kept believers from moving forward in the kingdom of God. Shame made the individual fear that he would be rejected. Shame made one afraid that he would be mocked and that he would be powerless. Shame made the community members terrified that their true self would be exposed and ultimately, they would be abandoned. Ole taught that Jesus Himself was profoundly discredited, His followers were scattered, and that He failed utterly. He became shame. Satan tries to get the individual to the resurrection by hiding the shame but, according to Ole, true disciples must confess their sinful behavior, embrace it, and thereby overcome their shame. Ole used the scripture passage from James 5:16a, "Confess your faults one to another, and pray one for another, that ye may be healed," to convince his followers that they must confess their disgraceful experiences to one other and see through the lie that others will abandon them when their shameful past is revealed.

Ole pronounced that the individual confessions would be conducted at what he called "hot seats" and persuaded his followers that it would create a group of people who could admit their weakness and allow their neediness to bind them together with one another. From Ole's perspective, hot seats would only be dreaded if the individual was shame-based. He wanted his disciples to arrive at a place where there was nothing left to confess, where they were totally transparent with one another and where they could totally trust each other.

Before the first hot seat took place, Ole told his group to make a list of everything they had done in their past of which they were ashamed. Each individual was to write down all of his or her earliest memories or experiences of shame. Ole arranged for the group to spend the weekend at a retreat center at Lake Texoma where the chronicle of each member's wrongdoings would be read out loud.

The first person to go through this horrendous experience was Dick. Dick prided himself on being creative and artistic, and he had worked hard all week preparing for that weekend. He was thrilled to be the first person to describe his past to the others and unveiled the collage he had made to illustrate his life. The collage was a visualization of the most intimate details of his life and had pictures of beautiful women, some naked, along with pictures symbolizing highs and lows in his career and in other aspects of his life. Dick explained his deepest feelings, using his artwork as a visual aid.

Then Ole began doing psychic surgery on him. "That collage is a piece of shit, Dick! I asked you people to be real, to be honest, but you can't do it. You talk about all the women in your life, but that's only a way to boast about your manhood. The truth is you have a deep-seated fear that you are, in fact, a homosexual. You have been covering up your homosexuality all your life by sleeping with women. You have to face your fears, Dick. You may be a homosexual, and if so, you are without hope. The scriptures declare that sodomites have no part in the kingdom of God. You are in serious trouble, my friend." Ole continued to bombard him until it seemed that all of his horrible secrets, his fears, and insecurities were brought to light. Dick's treasured collage was denigrated, and he was ridiculed for even making it. In fact, he continued to be mocked for years for having made this artwork.

The hot seats were gruesome, torturous events, both for the person on the hot seat as well as the other participants. The stated purpose was to free you from your past, free you from the things that were hindering you from entering the kingdom of God. In practice, however, they had the effect of changing the participant's perception of himself, reinterpreting his life history, and transforming his worldview by replacing it with Ole's. No one challenged Ole's insights. Though others would pile on and point out the contradictions and faults of the person being hot-seated, Ole kept tight control of the sessions and was the sole arbitrator and judicator of which insights were genuine, who had permission to speak, and, ultimately, when the person being hot-seated was sufficiently broken.

Each round of the hot seats had a different theme. Ole would expound on some type of false worship mentioned in the Old Testament, relate it to some aspect of psychology, and apply it to his audience. For example, the worship of the molten images had to do with the way we are programmed to respond emotionally to certain stimuli. If a person tended to become angry when confronted, that was a form of idolatry, which was preventing the individual from experiencing the true knowledge and worship of God. If, instead, one responded with fear to the same stimulus, that person was still an idolater, but the molten image had taken a different form than it had in the other person. Either way, the individual was not depending on God and was, therefore, under the curse. Regardless of what the stated theme was, the hot seats became psychic contests between the person who was on point and Ole, with Ole using every verbal assault imaginable to cause the person to break. Ole, of course, interpreted this as God and Satan contending for the soul of the person in question, with Ole leading the army of the Lord. It was a contest in which, by Ole's own admission, everything was permissible. There were no rules, no sense of fair play. After all, this was a battle for the soul.

To understand the kind of manipulation Ole was capable of on the hot seats, consider what happened to Diane. Diane and her mother started attending Trinity's Bible studies during her early adolescent years. Her mother left the group while she was still a teenager, but Diane continued to maintain a connection, sometimes sneaking off to attend Bible study against her mother's wishes. Trinity discouraged her from doing this while she was still under eighteen and living at home with her mother, but as soon as she turned eighteen, she married an older man in the group named Tony and took her place among the other members. In spite of her marriage, it was Ole's attention and approval that she craved more than anything. Ole found her neediness contemptible.

Diane worked in the flower shop of a funeral home. Her wedding was held in the chapel located on the grounds of the cemetery. During one of her hot seats, Ole said that because Diane and Tony were married at Restland Cemetery, this illustrated her obsession with death. As Diane began to squirm and tried to explain her reasoning, Ole began his attack. "You are a very disturbed young woman. You are bloodthirsty — the most macabre person I've ever met. I am sick unto death of you, Diane. You have been eating my flesh all your life." (This was Trinity Foundation jargon which meant that she was sustaining herself by trying to have Ole's approval rather than God's.) "I am leaving you to the others in the group because you are just gaining strength from my presence in the room."

Ole left the room, and the others lambasted Diane with their insights into her sins and shortcomings. This went on for quite some time, but she still would not break. Then, Ole came back in the house with a large butcher knife that had been used to cut up watermelon earlier in the day. He lay on the floor with the knife to his chest and threatened to kill himself right then and there unless she broke. The others were crying, praying, and begging Diane to repent so Ole would not have to kill himself. One former member, Dave, who was present at this hot seat recalled, "We believed that Ole would kill himself if Diane didn't break. If he had to do that as an act of laying down his own life for her, he would." At first, Diane just smirked at Ole and told him to quit. Ole told her he was quite serious. The group prayed and prayed for her to understand, for her heart not to be so hardened. Seeing Ole with the knife to his chest, Diane finally began to cry, pleaded with him not to do it, and begged for repentance. At last, she had broken.

It was Ole's role to discern the true meaning of any event described during each person's hot seat, and it was always stated in a way to make that person realize his or her total depravity. He would tell people that the Holy Spirit could not have anything to do with them because they were too evil, and that they had no hope of being saved. His favorite technique was to force one of his disciples into a state of despair so that he or she thought there was no possibility of salvation and then, when Ole felt that the person was sufficiently broken, he would turn it around. God had returned, and the person was safe, and he was a part of the Kingdom after all.

Ole had an uncanny talent for remembering scriptures and using them to support his opinions. He often quoted obscure passages from the Old Testament, which were unfamiliar to most people. According to several former members, Ole had an ability to read these scriptures in such a way that the person to whom he was talking felt like it had been written specifically for him. And many times he did not even have to look up the passage; he just quoted it from memory.

"Ole was quite adept at using passages of scripture to break you down. He had an amazing ability to recall Bible verses, and then he would use this God-voice. It was very frightening and it seemed that God was talking directly to you," recalled Doug.

Doug told of an especially painful hot seat from the mid 1980s when the group was meeting on Wentwood Street in north Dallas.

"Ole was just extraordinary at pulling out passages. I remember one hot seat where he quoted some stuff from Deuteronomy. He told me, 'thou shalt betroth a wife, and another man shall lie with her: ... thy daughters shall be given unto another people, ... he shall be the head, and thou shalt be the tail. Moreover all these curses shall come upon thee, and shall pursue thee, and overtake thee, till thou be destroyed; because thou hearkenedst not unto the voice of the Lord thy God, to keep his commandments and his statutes which he commanded thee" (Deuteronomy 28:30–45).

"And then several months later, Ole's prophecies came true. My wife left me for another man, divorced me, and took my three daughters to Florida to live."

I asked Doug if he had thought that Ole possessed remarkable spiritual discernment.

"Absolutely. We all did. When Ole's voice is the only one you hear, when his theology begins to penetrate your mind so that all previous truth and beliefs are buried, when his prophecies come true, it reinforced our belief that he understood the supernatural and could discern things that others could not.

"Ole would bust me about the fact that I did not speak in tongues, like that was a spiritual failing on my part. Ole had all of these spiritual manifestations, which he implied made him superior to everyone else. He was constantly quoting the apostle Paul, 'I thank God that I speak in tongues more than you all.'"

The hot seats had the effect of convincing individuals that they could not trust their own minds or feelings and causing them to doubt their very sense of reality. People would often bring up humiliating experiences from their childhoods—perhaps hoping for the promise of freedom from shame that was the recurrent theme in the hot seats—only to have these experiences reinterpreted in a way that caused them deeper shame. Doug recounted sharing the following incident while on a hot seat: "One time, when I was in the second grade, I was holding the flag for the Pledge of Allegiance and I didn't know my fly was down. Somehow, the flagpole got inside my pants. I was in front of a whole auditorium of kids. Of course, everyone has some embarrassing memories of events that happened to them in the process of growing up. These incidents are still painful to remember—but whatever you talked about, whatever you confessed, Ole always put a different spin on it. In this case, he said that I was actually an exhibitionist. I knew my fly was open and I purposefully flashed the whole auditorium of kids. I was an evil sinner and had been since birth."

The rationale for the hot seats was that they served as a vehicle to help the members of Trinity Foundation experience the freedom and joy that were their rightful inheritance as believers in Christ. The normal state for a disciple of Jesus should be freedom and joy, but there are these "imaginations and every high thing that exalts itself against the knowledge of God" that get in the way. The hot seats were held to redeem the members from the stumbling blocks which prevented them from being fully who they were meant to be in Christ.

Doug observed, "Ole does not understand that the legacy of the hot seats was fear and not freedom. Ole would say that by taking us through the process of breaking, he was bringing us into a place of freedom, but the hot seats brought no freedom. They brought cowering submission from the members and ever-increasing control for Ole. Through them Ole formed a body of people who felt fearful, powerless, and dependent upon him and the rest of the group. It was a systematic way to destroy people's egos and strip them of any sense of self-worth."

In justifying the hot seats, Ole told the group that people are like an unprogrammed computer when they are born. The only things written on the computer program is what God originally placed there, but then your parents hit on the keys and type their programs. And then others, such as your relatives, your babysitters, your friends, your teachers, etc., program their input. By the time you reach adulthood, you have a stack of floppy disks ten-feet-high through which all information is processed, and what comes out is totally different from what God intended. There may be some truth to Ole's premise here, but the problem was that the programming, which people received from their parents and from society — some of it no doubt destructive — was replaced not with God's programming, but with Ole's.

Back to my interview with Mark:

"But Mark, if the hot seats were so emotionally terrifying, why did people stay? Why didn't they get up and walk out?" I asked, still trying to understand the dynamics of the hot seats.

"Because at that time, there was a strong belief that we were doing the right thing. None of us could see the damage. Ole convinced us that the shameful events in our past were the things that defined us now — defined our false worship. Where we had kinks or sexual compulsions, they were still controlling us in some way.

"We believed that we were in a spiritual, life-and-death struggle for the soul of the individual who was on the hot seat. If each of us did not repent, we would be forever banished to hell. We were engaged in this spiritual warfare. There was a grand fight going on between God and Satan, a battle for our souls. The other people in the room would be crying, wailing, speaking in tongues, falling on the ground, and begging God to have mercy on your soul. It was an intense experience, sometimes lasting until dawn."

Another former member, Paula, described her experience: "At my first hot seat, I started telling something about my childhood and Ole interrupted to say, 'That's not true. None of that is true. Your dad never did any of that to you. You and your mom controlled your dad and hen-pecked him to death.' I was so freaked out about the whole hot seat thing that I burst into tears and agreed to everything he said even though looking back on it later I was like, 'Why did I agree?'

"Ole drilled it into each of our heads that we were each the chief of sinners. So I always thought that whatever accusation Ole made against me, he must be right. I am guilty. The hot seats tore you down to where you were nothing but a mass of jelly. If you had any confidence or self-esteem when you began the hot seats, you sure weren't going to have any when it ended.

"At one hot seat I was told to go outside and walk around. I felt like the lowest of the low and not even God could forgive me. I thought I was the hardest-hearted, most sinful person in the world and there was no hope of salvation for me. If I could have found a way to commit suicide that night, I would have done it.

"And it wasn't just Ole. Everybody was joining in on the attack and I thought that all those things Ole said about me must be true because no one contradicted him. I was convinced that if the others didn't agree with Ole, they would say something. Years later, I began to understand why they didn't speak out. But when I was going through it, I concluded that everyone here loved me, and they would let me know if something wasn't right with what Ole was saying.

"I know it sounds odd that I would allow someone to abuse me that way, but I was convinced that unless I went through the hot seat, I would never be able to see what was keeping me from being real, keeping me from fellowship, keeping me from being who I was supposed to be in Christ. You submit to those things because there are things about yourself that you believe you do not perceive accurately. You think you can't see yourself correctly.

"Ole would quote that verse in the Bible about the heart being deceitful above all else. Only Ole and the group could see the real me, so I had to confess all my secret sins. Those secret sins were keeping me from knowing God and entering the body of Christ—and my unwillingness to confess was keeping others from becoming part of the body of Christ. Their blood was on my hands.

"I was a believer before I ever started going to the Trinity Foundation. I loved the Lord with all my heart, so I wanted to do whatever I needed to do. I loved the Father, and I wanted more than anything to be a servant to Him. So if that meant I had to get on the hot seat and spill my guts in order for me to be an instrument for Him to use, I was willing to do it. That was my motivation."

People confessed to pedophilia, voyeurism, bestiality, incest, and prostitution—every imaginable thing. Even if one had only thought about these things, he was still guilty. For example, if a man "lusted" after a woman other than his wife, he had committed adultery just as much as if he had actually acted out the deed.

It did not matter what you had done or what you wrote down on your list, Ole was going to make it about something else. From Ole's perspective, you had not repented from it and you were going to hell unless you could repent right now. The future was irrelevant, and only the present mattered. You were either saved at that moment, or you were damned at that moment—and right then, unless you saw the serious nature of your sins and the terrible crisis you were in before

God, you would not—could not—be saved. You were a reprobate—eternally damned.

Mark left the Trinity Foundation several years before the hot-seat era to pursue a career in radio. He worked in several major markets around the country before moving to Seattle to work for a radio station there as a disc jockey. During this time, Doug started sending him tapes of Ole's Bible studies. Mark recalls, "Seattle was a particularly horrendous experience for me. In the midst of it all, my grandfather died. I had a phone conversation with Ole, who in his typical fashion quoted a scripture from one of the prophets in the Old Testament, 'Mark, you are putting your money in a bag full of holes for God to come and blow on.' That sounded like a bad deal, so I decided I had better go back to Trinity. I was about twenty-eight years old then; I had been gone for about eight years. Very much the prodigal son, I guess. I returned [to Dallas] specifically to go to Trinity, but when I came back I found a much heavier, much darker, more intense place than the one I had left years before.

"Ole had just started the second round of hot seats, and I guess you could say that he was reveling in his newfound power and authority. He had never had anything that had allowed him to truly control the members of the group prior to that. You could tell this was like a big discovery to him.

"And it had become a regular thing. Everybody was going to have a hot seat. 'Judgment must first begin at the house of the Lord' was Ole's justification. None of us really understood what that meant, but I was put on the hot seat just a few days after I got back. Ole couldn't wait. It was even joked about—'Ole can't wait to get Mark on the hot seat'—so, I was on the hot seat before I knew it. I remember experiencing complete bewilderment and excruciating discomfort, but I was willing to endure it because there was such a strong belief that we were doing the right thing. None of us had yet seen the damage that the hot seats would do to us spiritually and emotionally."

The hot-seat event was further reinforced by the behavior of the group. As one member, Dave, explained, "I was surrounded by my friends, people who had become my family, who I believed loved and cared for me. If the whole group believed that Ole's insights into my inner being were true, how could I doubt it? It must be right because everyone who loved me thought it was right."

It was also absolutely forbidden for anyone to defend or even secretly sympathize with the individual who was on the hot seat. If you did, you were brutally attacked because you were in an alliance with him, and you were preventing him from repenting, thereby exiling him permanently to hell.

One set of hot seats was about the "high-place identities." Ole would quote Ephesians 6:12 where the Bible says, "For we wrestle not against flesh and blood, but against principalities, against powers, against the rulers of the darkness of this world, against spiritual wickedness in high places." Ole taught that the high-place identities were the satanic counterfeits of the individual's office in the Body of Christ. Just as every believer has an office in the Body of Christ, he has a function in the body of Satan. The service to Satan can only be a perversion of what the individual's service should be to God.

Ole taught that during our youth we learn a certain role that we use to manipulate our world. The high-place identities are the roles that we use to get what we want, our flesh employing a specific evil persona to try to make things happen, in contrast to our true identity in Jesus, which is trusting in God the Father for everything.

To see things in terms of the metaphorical reality that Ole constructed was to see in the Spirit—to see reality from God's perspective. To the people at the Trinity Foundation, the allegorical myth that Ole created about the high-place identity was reality. Ole would say, "If you can see in the Spirit, you are like a Jezebel, a high priestess, controlling everything, pulling all the strings, etc. etc." According to Ole, Jezebel was the most evil one, and she would inevitably try to kill the prophet of God. Ole labeled many of the women in the group with the high-place identity of Jezebel, and at one point, there were five Jezebels in the group. This Jezebel identity would try to silence the man of God, just as the Jezebel in the Old Testament tried to do with Elijah by attempting to kill him. The implication was that Ole was Elijah, the prophet, trying to bring the word of God to the people. Any attempts to challenge Ole were just proof that one was a "Jezebel."

Along with Mark, Moira was one of the few former members who could talk about the hot seats. Although she had left the Trinity Foundation ten years ago, the pain she had experienced was still very fresh. Tears streamed down her face as she recalled the experience. "My first hot seat was about my high-place identity. I was a witch. I weaved spells and incantations to get what I wanted. I was the kind of witch who was like a queen. It was as if I was sitting there and all my subjects were males, and their whole job was to perform sexual favors. This was said in front of everybody else! I felt so dirty and humiliated.

"We had been told to make a list of all the things we had done of which we were ashamed. So I made my list, and then I had to say it in front of everybody. The intention was that it wouldn't leave the room, so whatever you knew about that person or whatever he had done, you couldn't tell anybody else. But when you open up like that in front of a whole bunch of people, even though you consider them your family, it does something to you psychologically. It makes you more vulnerable. It makes you feel less in control of your own life. And it makes you feel that you have put your life in the hands of the group, not just Ole's, but everyone's. So when you get to that point where you pour out your heart, saying all these awful terrible things that you have done and how you are so ashamed of who you are, things you have never told anyone, you're already broken, and you're already vulnerable."

Moira continued to explain, "My second hot seat was much worse. Ole said he had not discerned my high-place identity correctly. I wasn't a witch; I was a failed high priestess."

"What did that mean?" I asked.

"I wasn't even a high priestess. I was a *failed* high priestess. The failed high priestess is someone who aspires to be a high priestess, but never gets there. I was like a lady-in-waiting who was always there, ready and willing to be the bride, but was never going to be the bride. I was a failed high priestess waiting for the husband, but the husband was not going to pick me. Any hope for holiness or redemption or anything was not going to happen to me. It also meant that I had this potential to be something great, to do something successful, something more fulfilling, but that I would never make it. There was no hope for me."

"Did you cry?" I asked.

"Oh, yeah. I remember that I had this blue jean skirt on, and I kept wiping my face and my tears on that skirt, and it was soaking wet. I cried and cried. I was devastated. At some point, the hot seat experience ended, and people came over to me and hugged me. It's hard to explain, but you feel numb, and you continue to feel numb for days later. The few minutes of hugging weren't enough to compensate for the hours you were ridiculed and attacked."

After the ordeal of a hot seat, people would report a type of disassociation—a feeling of numbness that lasted for three or four days. If brokenness is the ultimate good, then the best one can do is to break people—and that's what Ole believed he was called by God to do. People's spirits had to be broken. Ole would quote Psalm 51:17 "The sacrifices of God are a broken spirit: a broken and a contrite heart, O God, thou wilt not despise." Breaking a person's spirit was a good thing in Ole's economy.

The goal of these marathon sessions was to break whoever was on the hot seat, and the sessions would continue—often for many hours—until the person broke. Ole convinced the group members that he had the keys to the kingdom—and that their very salvation was on the line unless they broke.

Dave recalled that, "If you crossed Ole in some minor detail, you were subject to being "hot-seated" at any time. Someone would manifest a bad attitude and Ole would call everybody in the room, and boom, one of the members was on the hot seat. Even during the Bible studies, hot seats would flare up constantly. Anybody who stood up to Ole at any time during the hot-seat era would be crushed."

Mark recalled his last night in the group, "My last hot seat: I had been dating a woman, and Ole was not happy about my relationship with her, because he wanted me to be with my former wife, Crystal. Crystal and I had only been married six months, and that was over ten years ago, but Ole did everything humanly possible to manipulate our getting back together. Ole had Crystal admit in Bible study that she was in love with me. Talk about your peer pressure! But I was dating Nicole, and that just screwed up everything.

"Nicole left the group, and Ole put me on the hot seat one night in Bible study and blamed me for Nicole leaving the group, which I thought was fascinating because she was the last person I wanted to see leave the group. In my opinion, Nicole left the group because she got tired of Ole's abuse. But anyway, I was in my Bible study group, and Ole went around the room to ask the other members what punishment

I should have for causing Nicole to leave—and for being a "screw-up." My supposed buddies each had an idea, which ranged from picking up trash to washing dishes in the Lair. It was quite an assortment of punishment.

"I remember sitting in the corner of the room, in the chair, in the typical hot-seat position. Ole held up his Bible and he said, 'Mark, you would say that I know this book pretty well, wouldn't you?' And I said, 'Yes, Ole, I would say you know it very well.' Then he said, 'I don't see anything in it that can help you.' And he snapped the Bible closed.

"And with that I was gone. I was still physically there, but I began to float above the room. All I could think of was that there was no hope for me."

Amanda distinctly remembered Mark's last night at Trinity, "I do remember this vividly. Ole was in his chair and I was sitting two people to his right. Mark was on the floor near Ole's ottoman. Ole was teaching about the doctrine of election. He said that we couldn't choose God, because if we choose God, we are doing it for selfish reasons, so we have no participation at all in our relationship with God. Individuals have no say in it—you can't decide or determine if you are going to be one of the elect, the chosen, or one of the saved. Now, Ole never used the word save. That comes strictly from my Baptist upbringing, but this particular Bible study night, Ole made the comment to Mark, 'Well, maybe you are not one of the chosen. There is no hope for you.'

"I will never forget the look on Mark's face—he was stunned. Totally shocked and devastated by what came out of Ole's mouth. Mark truly believed that Ole had the words of God. So for Ole to say to Mark that he wasn't one of the elect, he was saying that he was damned. It was a horrible, spiritually devastating thing to say to someone. I can still see the look on Mark's face."

That night was Mark's last time at the Trinity Foundation. The next morning he packed some clothes in a laundry bag and acted as if he was leaving to wash his clothes. With only his laundry bag, he left and went to his parents' home. His mother and father sensed that he was on the verge of a mental breakdown and immediately took him to a psychologist. After hearing Mark's experience, the psychologist asked him to sit in the waiting area while he met with his parents. Mark recalled, "That was the first time my parents were truly alerted to the fact that I was in a cult and the danger of that. And boy, they came out of that room white as ghosts. They were completely freaked out. And then, I was sent to a psychiatrist and as I talked to him, I began to cry. The psychologist had recommended that I be on a suicide watch and that I not be left alone because I was so depressed. So, when I started talking to the psychiatrist I started to cry. I must have cried for about two days, maybe a week. I don't remember. Just remember crying all the time."

The formal hot seats were eventually abandoned in the early 1990s for a number of reasons. First of all, they were no longer necessary. Ole had attained the level of control he desired over the people with whom he was in direct contact, his core followers, and he did not need to break them any further. He probably sensed that to do so would be counterproductive, since people who have been broken too many times become more helpless and dependent than even Ole wanted them to be. Second, with the advent of the televangelist investigations, the focus of Trinity Foundation turned outward. Ole became less concerned with transforming his disciples and more focused on changing the visible Christian church in America. He had trained his little army of followers, and he was ready now to lead them into war. Third, there was the case of Sean.

Sean was a sensitive, young man whom Ole pushed too far one night on a hot seat. Sean had a psychotic break shortly after his hot seat, becoming so obsessed with washing his hands that he did so until they bled. Of course, neither Ole nor anyone else at Trinity Foundation could admit that his hot seat was the reason Sean "went crazy." Ole expended a great deal of effort to convince everyone that Sean's problems were the results of a bad reaction to Naprosyn, which had been prescribed to him for a work-related injury to his shoulder. Naprosyn is a non-steroidal, anti-inflammatory drug similar to aspirin, but Ole was able to intimidate Sean's insurance company into treating his emotional problem as though it were something related to his work injury and the drug that had been prescribed for it.

Ole never admitted any responsibility for what he had done to Sean, but the hot seats stopped shortly after that particular episode. Though he is probably unwilling to acknowledge his role in this tragic situation, I suspect that in his heart of hearts Ole knows what he did.

By the time I arrived in 1993, the formal hot seats had been discontinued. For the people who had been through them so many times, they were no longer necessary. Ole could take them back to that moment of abject terror and fear of both abandonment and damnation anytime he wanted to with just the sound of his voice—sometimes just a look. Ole had been an expert hypnotist before becoming a religious believer, and some of the former members thought that what Ole did with his voice was a form of hypnotism. Moreover, once you have revealed all of your deepest, darkest secrets, you are left feeling vulnerable. Members remembered that Ole had taken notes during their hot seats and a record had been kept. The knowledge of this file, along with the memory of the hot seats, was sufficient for a very effective form of social control.

CHAPTER 7

✝

Believers in the Hands of an Angry Cult Leader

One of the most famous sermons ever preached was Jonathan Edwards' "Sinners in the Hands of an Angry God," which began with this ominous statement: "There is nothing that keeps wicked men at any one moment out of hell, but the mere pleasure of God."

This sermon preached in 1741 set the standard for "hellfire and brimstone." Edwards' six-hour sermon was so powerful that men and women cried and begged for mercy, and clung to the seats of their pews out of fear that they might be thrown into hell at any moment. Reading his sermon and the effect that it had on his listeners helped me to understand the impact that Ole had when he had his followers on the "hot seat."

The core of Ole's doctrine is best summed up by Jonathan Edwards' well-known sermon. The following excerpt from "Sinners in the Hands of an Angry God" succinctly describes Ole's teaching on God:

The God that holds you over the pit of hell, much in the same way as one holds a spider, or some loathsome insect, over the fire, abhors you, and is dreadfully provoked; His wrath towards you burns like fire; He looks upon you as worthy of nothing else but to be cast into the fire; He is of purer eyes than to bear to have you in His sight; you are ten thousand times more abominable in His eyes than the most hateful venomous serpent is in ours. [1]

That was the essence of Trinity Foundation and its doctrine. Jonathan Edwards was a great preacher and had exceptional power over his listeners, but whereas Edwards balanced his doctrine of God as being both a wrathful god, and at the same time, the God of mercy willing that no man should perish, Ole's doctrine was substantially weighted on the side of the wrath of God.

One of Ole's teachings was that God abhorred the human race. Though most Christian theologians would agree that God hates man's sinfulness, they would not agree that the Bible portrays God as hating mankind. I recall Ole ridiculing Bill Bright's evangelical tract, *The Good News*, and saying, "It's not Good News, it's Bad News!"

Over the years Doug had told me bits and pieces about a time when he was on a hot seat and Ole had read the book of Jude to him in such a way that Doug was totally convinced that it has been written specifically for him. Doug always described it as one of the most gruesome hot seats that had occurred up to that point in Trinity's history. Early in my search to understand the impact that the hot seats had on former members, I mentioned to my husband that I had read the book of Jude earlier that day and did not understand why it had been so disturbing to him.

In an attempt to help me understand, Doug retrieved his Bible, opened it to the book of Jude, and began reading out loud in the Ole voice: "*For there are certain men crept in unawares, who were before of old ordained to this condemnation, ungodly men, turning the grace of our Lord into lasciviousness, and denying the only Lord God, and our Lord Jesus Christ."*

Doug paused in his reading and said, "Wendy, when Ole read that to me he was stating very clearly that I was one of those ungodly men who had crept in amongst the believers. I was not a real believer. I was just pretending. He was using his wrath-of-God voice and looking at me with those eyes that felt like they were penetrating into my very soul. It was frightening."

Doug continued to read from Jude: "*I will therefore put you in remembrance, though ye once knew this, how that the Lord, having saved the people out of the land of Egypt, afterward destroyed them that believed not."*

Again, mimicking Ole's commentary, "God destroyed those who did not believe, Doug. After He saved the whole community, then He found out the ones who were sprinkled in among us who were not real believers and He destroyed them. I don't care whether you're an elder or not, Doug. It doesn't matter. God has condemned you to eternal damnation. He will not spare you."

At this point Doug strayed from the exact quote from the book of Jude recalling how he remembered Ole reading this passage to him: "'*Just like the angels who were rebellious, God has reserved everlasting chains under darkness for you. Even as Sodom and Gomorrah and the cities about them in like manner* ....' You, Doug, are as evil and wicked as the men of Sodom. And, make no mistake, God will destroy you and you will suffer the vengeance of eternal fire.

"'*Likewise also these filthy dreamers defile the flesh, despise dominion, and speak evil of dignities.*' Ole then said, 'In all of your rebellion, that's exactly what you are doing, Doug. You are a filthy dreamer and you despise the fact that I am your covering.'" Doug went on to explain to me, "I didn't have the Spirit. I had complained. I had opposed Ole. With that authoritative voice yelling at me, telling me how hopeless I was before God and that everything I did was just an attempt to save my own life. Ole told me that I knew nothing of repentance—nothing of what it meant to be a believer.

"'*But these speak evil of those things which they know not: but what they know naturally, as brute beasts, in those things they corrupt themselves. Woe unto them! For they have gone in the way of Cain, and ran greedily after the error of Balaam for reward, and perished in the gainsaying of Korah.*' Do you not understand, Doug? This is God's word to you. You are evil and you speak evil because you are not a true believer. You are a brute beast.

"'*These are spots in your feasts of charity, when they feast with you, feeding themselves without fear: clouds they are without water, carried about of winds; trees whose fruit withereth, without fruit, twice dead, plucked up by the roots; Raging waves of the sea, foaming out their own shame; wandering stars, to whom is reserved the blackness of darkness for ever.*' God sees you as a spot in this community. You are a cloud without water, Doug. You are twice dead and God has reserved the blackest of darkness for you.

"'*Mockers in the last days these be they who separate themselves. Having not the Spirit*' (Doug's paraphrase of verse 18). I remember Ole looking me straight in the eye when he read that part. He had said things before about me not having the Spirit because I didn't and couldn't speak in tongues. I wasn't charismatic; therefore, in Ole's mind I wasn't saved, I wasn't one of the chosen ones. The darkness of condemnation and eternal fire was reserved for me because I didn't have the Spirit.

"I look at it now and can say, 'This is not talking about me,' but to have had the book of Jude read to me by someone with the voice and wrath of God and he purports that God is talking directly to me ..." Doug's voice trailed off. "Ole was telling me that the wrath of God burned against me. There was no hope for me. Now, as I am reading this, I wonder why I didn't say something like, 'Ole, you're full of it.' But when you are on the hot seat, there is no possible way to muster the ego-strength to even think that thought. Over time, I had been systematically worn down and my psyche had been chipped away at for years. I had been crushed like powder during hot seats and had been broken again and again.

"Not only was there no ego-strength to oppose Ole, but also, in some sense I had become completely immersed in the cosmology of the Trinity Foundation. I totally had bought into Ole's theological constructs. For me to have told Ole he was wrong would have been like thinking that someone living in medieval Europe who had been excommunicated from the church could confront the bishop. There is only one church. The bishop is the Vicar of Christ—you can't oppose him. It not only wouldn't occur to you, it absolutely couldn't occur to you.

"I had truly bought into the Trinity belief system. I believed that Ole was the prophet of God who had brought the knowledge of the true faith back into the world. There was no possible way I could have said to him, 'Ole, you are wrong.'"

Doug continued reading from the book of Jude: "'*Keep yourselves in the love of God, looking for the mercy of our Lord Jesus Christ unto eternal life.*' Ole sprinkled a little mercy stuff in the end, but by this time, I was spiritually in shock. It was like the time when Bill Clinton allegedly raped that woman and bit her lip and when he was leaving, he looked back at her and said, 'You ought to put some ice on that.' Well, that seems like he had some concern for her, but he had just raped her. That little bit of niceness was not enough to overcome what he had just done to her.

"Wendy, you asked me why the book of Jude caused such a traumatic response when Ole read it to me. Do you understand now? Can you see how terrifying it was? I have a problem with God because of Jude. This book shouldn't even be in the Bible. I regret that I had to read you that book because I was just getting back to the point where I could start reading the Bible again. Now it will probably be another year before I can try reading it again."

My heart began to ache once again for my dear husband who had experienced so much pain at the hands of our angry cult leader. I knew that reading the book of Jude aloud to me had caused Doug to relive Ole's execution of his soul and had revived those old memories of terror, of overwhelming fear at the prospect of not being a true believer and consequently being damned forever.

As often happened during the period when Doug was struggling to understand the experience he had at Trinity Foundation, he defended Ole. "As far as the rationale of the hot seats was concerned, Ole was trying to get his followers to the place where they experientially felt total damnation, and then in that place, to somehow or another provide them with the grace and mercy of God so as to have some understanding that it was only by the grace and mercy of God that salvation was possible. Ole was so hard on us because he wanted us to understand that if God did to us what we deserved, then the next step we took would be into the pit and we would never stop falling until we hit the lake of fire. In Ole's mind, he was pulling us from the fire of hell, saving us from the wrath of God."

"What did you do after Ole read the book of Jude to you?" I asked.

"I was sent out into the dark night. Ole told me to go outside and think about my sinful spirit and unrepentant heart. We were at a church retreat center in the middle of the piney woods in East Texas. I walked around in the pitch dark and prayed and prayed for God's mercy.

"When I came back in, the room was quiet. People were deep in prayer for my soul. Ole told everyone to keep praying because the Holy Spirit was circling the room try-ing to find someone who would lay down his or her life for me. Finally, Garth came over to me and said, 'I lay down my life for Doug.' He began to pray over me. Until that moment, I had been anesthetized by the fear, almost in a state of shock, but when he began praying, the numbness began to fade and I started sobbing. Then people started falling on the floor and crying.

"Once I broke, crying on the floor in the fetal position, everyone hugged me and told me that they loved me. There was a great feeling of release and mercy now that I had repented and joined the family of God. Of course, it was the group—and Ole, in particular—who could withdraw this 'grace' at any time, and each of us intuitively felt that.

"Years after the hot seat experiences, one of the most insightful statements was what Paula said: 'You get beaten up for six hours, then hugged for five minutes, and that's sup-posed to balance the equation.' You would have six hours of pounding, putting you down, hammering on you, thrashing you, tearing you apart, and then you would break and there would be ten minutes of the love fest where everyone would hug and say, 'Praise God. Hallelujah.' Then it was over, and everyone went home.

"Well, the ratio was six hours to ten minutes. Six hours of hell and ten minutes of grace. That sums up the whole Trinity Foundation experience.

"It's like the husband who beats up his wife, and then brings her a bouquet of roses thinking that this would make up for giving her a black eye. The batterer believes that he has made it up to her, and that's what Ole thought. 'I love you and I'm only doing this because I want you to be a better person.' In the mind of the wife-beater, he loves her, and he is only trying to make her a better wife. Ole, too, thought that he was doing the right thing. He believed that he loved his followers.

"There is a place for correction and exhortation. There is a place for discipline. But the overwhelming message of the New Testament is love and forgiveness. Why wasn't that the overwhelming message of Ole's doctrine? That's the message of Romans. The first part of the book of Romans talks about the carnal mind, but by the time you get to chapter eight, Paul says, 'Who can separate us from the love of God?' Not even our own carnal minds. Ole did not exert any time or energy in building people up or edifying them."

"Wendy, why did you prod me into reading the book of Jude like that?" Doug asked. "When you asked, 'What's wrong with the book of Jude?' were you serious?"

"Yeah, I was."

"Why, because you only read the first verse?"

"No, because I read the ending: *Now unto him that is able to keep you from falling, and to present you faultless before the presence of his glory with exceeding joy. To the only wise God our Savior, be glory and majesty, dominion and power, both now and ever.*'"

Doug replied, "If Ole read that part, if he ever got to the grace and mercy verses of the book of Jude, I didn't hear it. I was shell-shocked."

One of the greatest tragedies of the Trinity Foundation was that it produced a spirit of fear and bondage in its members. Romans 8:15 says that we have not been given the spirit of bondage again to fear, but rather the Spirit of adoption, whereby we cry, "Abba, Father."

It is hard to see the merciful arms of a loving God when you are in the hands of an angry cult leader. The aching pains and scars from the past clouded our memory of the God of Grace and could only be erased by His boundless love and mercy. We both still had a long way to go in the healing process and we prayed to know again the unfailing love and peace of the Father.

CHAPTER 8

Twisted Doctrine

"*They went out from us, but they were not of us; for if they had been of us, they would no doubt have continued with us*" (1 John 2:19a). If you had been at Trinity Foundation for any length of time, you would have heard this verse used repeatedly as an explanation when someone left the group. Those who "went out" (i.e., did not remain in the community) "were not of us" — "us" being the Trinity Foundation. Those individuals who left the group never really belonged — never were true believers. From Ole's perspective, the community was the body of Christ, the Bride — the only thing that God cared about. Ole believed that although many people had passed through the doors of the Trinity Foundation, only the true disciples had stayed.

The real believer was one who had begun in the faith, who had tasted of the Word of God, and who continued to abide (stay in the community). "Once you have tasted of the good Word of God, and the world to come, nothing else in the universe can ever satisfy you," was what we were told. In not continuing in the "faith," in falling away from the Trinity Foundation, we were destined for a life of misery.

Ole often talked about the "almost disciple," referring to a member of Trinity Foundation who began the process of laying down his life for the brethren and the community, but who eventually left. The "almost disciple" always failed God's test. He or she would become hurt or angry over some offense, or could not tolerate the constant reproofs that came from Ole and the elders, so the almost-disciple would leave. Conversely, the true believers who had the same complaints, the same problems, the same reprimands, continued in the doctrine and, because of God's faith, they endured. Whatever had caused them chastisement or what they perceived as some annoyance, the true believer allowed God to transform them into something precious.

In the Trinity world, leaving or withdrawing was spiritually the same as murdering your brother or sister. In Ole's interpretation of scripture, the Bible teaches, "If you say you love God and hate your brother, you are a liar. And if you withdraw from your brothers and sisters in Christ for any reason, you are saying you hate them, and therefore, you are saying you hate God" (see 1 John 3–4). In Ole's estimation, there was never any justification for withdrawing or leaving.

They went out from us, but they were not of us; for if they had been of us, they would no doubt have continued with us. When those nagging doubts entered your mind about the truth of the Trinity Foundation, this verse would echo in your mind, and you would think, "If I leave, I must not be a true believer." This erroneous belief was further emphasized by the way that the group treated people who left. Since former members had chosen not to abide in the community, they were "of the world" — consequently, whether they were true believers was questionable.

After I left the Trinity Foundation, I talked with a former member who had left the group several years before us. Matthew gave me some helpful advice: "When I first left, I knew I would not be able to think my way out of the doctrine. It is a closed system full of syllogisms, and if you accept these premises, then some of Ole's conclusions seem inescapable. It is like one of those monkey traps where the monkey reaches inside a box to grab a piece of banana, and then he cannot get away. Once he is holding the fruit, his hand is too big for him to withdraw it from the box. He is too dumb to realize than if he would simply let go of it, he could get his hand out easily and scamper away."

Matthew continued by saying, "The only way I was able to separate intellectually from the things we were taught at Trinity was to focus not upon the doctrine, but rather the practices of Trinity Foundation. That is why the most important book I read after I decided to leave was Steven Hassan's *Combatting Cult Mind Control*. Hassan believes that in examining a cult, it is less important to focus on what they teach than it is on what they *do*. This makes sense if you think about it, because cults teach many different things, but it is what they practice and their authoritarian structure that defines them as cults."

He had a point. Some of what Ole taught was mainstream Christian doctrine, and it was very difficult to extricate the good from the bad. Even though I left the foundation more than five years ago, I am still sorting through my belief system.

Ole thought of himself as an original thinker and pioneer when it came to discovering new spiritual insights. He often spoke contemptuously of people (such as Moses Maimonides, the brilliant Jewish scholar and teacher of the twelfth century) whom Ole dismissed as a mere "codifier," rather than an "innovator" like himself. Ole's disdain of systemization, however, spilled over into what he taught. Though he did have occasional insights, his lack of a formal theological education deprived him of the tools which he needed to organize his teaching into a coherent whole. Ole was not capable of achieving what someone like theologian Karl Barth did in putting together a comprehensive systematic theology.

This lack of systematization makes it difficult to critique Ole's teaching in an orderly way; however, it is possible to go through the points that he emphasized and look at them in terms of how they were used to reinforce his control over his followers. A fair examination of the primary teachings of the Trinity Foundation would include considering how these teachings were used to push the practices of the group in a cultic direction.

To Ole, the greatest of all heresies was what the modern church teaches—the doctrine of salvation of the isolated self—which he referred to as the doctrine of Ephraim. It was impossible, in his schema, for an individual to be saved apart from surrendering his identity—his individuality—to a "body" (i.e., a group of believers). In other words, if you were not a member of a body, you were not really walking as a Christian. This was the essence of the faith and the enlightenment that Ole had been given. According to Ole, everyone was either a vessel of wrath or a vessel of mercy—destined for either damnation or glory. If you had not forsaken "self," you were a vessel of wrath and were consequently unfit for the kingdom of God.

Ole repeatedly proclaimed that the modern church teaching on "salvation of the isolated believer" was contrary to everything that the Bible taught, and he admonished us to abandon modern Christianity's heresy. He would frequently lament the fact that the church today did not understand the basic truth that he knew. Ole often denounced the heretical teachings of the modern church with statements such as, "Salvation of the isolated self. Self-realization! That's the focus of Americana. The essence of American religion. Find that for me in scripture! To understand the mystery of God, we must abandon modern Christianity's doctrine of the isolated self. God doesn't want any lone rangers." Ole believed that God did not deal with people as individuals, but only as a body, and therefore, to understand fully the mystery of God, we had to come to this spiritual enlightenment.

According to Ole, the love of God was only for Jesus and His Bride—not the human race. He did not love the individual, but He loved what that individual could become, which was a member of the Bride of Christ. The correct translation of the passage in John 3:16 which states, "God so loved the world that He gave his only begotten Son," Ole maintained, should be translated, "God so loved the Bride," with the Bride being the true church; however, evangelical Christianity did not have a true understanding of this passage and taught that God loved the individual.

Ole deplored the teaching that God loves the individual, and one of his frequent sayings was "God hates you." By this, he meant that God hates you "after the flesh." There was a distinction between you in the flesh and you in the spirit. In the flesh, you were self-seeking, isolated, and apart from God. The individual alone, striving for glory, was an affront to God. One could know nothing of the spiritual walk until experiencing the humility of being a part of a body and considering daily that the needs of other people were more important than one's own needs. It was the isolated self that refused to subordinate its life and agenda in order to be a part of a body that God truly hated. It was only the Bride of Christ that God cared about. God did not love man. Because God did not love the individual, but, in fact, hated him, it was absolute arrogance on man's part to think that the God of this universe would want to have a relationship with him. God's only desire was for a relationship with His Bride and only by becoming a part of the Bride could one hope to find salvation.

Of course, this meant there was no such thing as a personal relationship with God. Ole would often make fun of teachings from mainstream Christianity regarding salvation. Ole taught that the word *faith* was *rhema* in the Greek language and meant "that which one had already received." Every man has faith, and when he finally understands that, there's an electrical spark that takes place and he recognizes that Christ is already in him. In Ole's words, "You can't receive Jesus as your personal Savior. That's the dumbest thing that's ever been foisted on the human race. Christ is already in you."

Another evangelical teaching that Ole abhorred and often ridiculed was that "God loves you and has a wonderful plan for your life." Ole constantly mocked the modern church, specifically evangelicals, who proclaimed that the Gospel of Christ was good news. "That God loves you and wants you to have a wonderful life is a bunch of crap," exclaimed Ole. "God does not love the human race and does not have a wonderful plan for your life. The only purpose He has is for mankind to die and to be buried so that a new thing can be born—the Bride of Christ.

"God's design for your life is that you will die!" he would thunder. Ole proclaimed that God would do everything to make sure that your life as an individual in the world was a failure, including, he was fond of saying, "killing your dog." Ole taught that God would do anything to help you see that you, left to yourself, were a pathetic loser and your only hope was to "pick up the cross," or in another metaphor, "fall into the ground and die." In short, by God's grace, everything in your life would go wrong so that you would give up trying to make something of yourself and wholly give yourself to the service of the body (which turned out in practice to mean wholly giving yourself to the service of Ole).

The effect that this teaching had on members such as Anna, who grew up in a physically abusive family, was profoundly damaging. Anna had no problem believing this doctrine because she never saw a father as a loving and caring person. She struggled with self-loathing, and this teaching just validated that she was unworthy of the love of a heavenly father.

Amanda articulated how this specific doctrine impacted her. "Ole's teaching on God's hatred of the human race was something I absolutely believed during the time I was a member of Trinity Foundation; however, I now see that it was the most sinister distortion of the character of God and that it almost undermined my faith. I can also clearly see how this teaching and others similar to it that were forced upon us were used to destroy our sense of self-worth.

"For me, personally, the greatest issue was the manipulation of the Gospel to such an unhealthy extent that it was always pointed out how we were the greatest of all sinners. And if we were the greatest of all sinners, then we were whores. We were murderers. We were all of these sins known to man because we couldn't have done one without having done them all. That doctrine was emphatically taught, and during Bible studies, people would be called whores, sluts, and murderers. When one is told something over and over, he begins to believe it. In the process of trying to get us to the point where we did not see ourselves as separate beings, Ole took away that precious part of us that God created—our individuality. This teaching had the effect of severely damaging our self-esteem and kept us from the understanding of what it meant to be a child of God."

In Bible studies, the central message was the total depravity of man. It was important in the eyes of the teachers at Trinity Foundation for everyone to understand the fact that they were unredeemable sinners so almost every Bible study touched on this issue. Unless we completely understood how evil we were, we could not understand the true meaning of

Christ's death on the cross. Not only did we need to see how evil we were, but we also had to loathe everything that had anything to do with our individual "self." Until then, there could be no repentance. One of the primary problems with the doctrine that Ole taught was its imbalance and emphasis on the crucifixion of Christ. Ole taught that the true meaning of the cross was that when Christ died, all mankind died. He often quoted this scripture: "because we thus judge, that if one died for all, then were all dead" (2 Cor. 5:14).

"Picking up the cross" was another prominent theme in Bible studies. In Trinity Foundation's doctrine, the definition of picking up the cross meant total denial of self. The individual was to totally abandon any thought for self, which meant that he was not to give any importance to his reputation, possessions or lack thereof, no plans about tomorrow, or credence for emotions or feelings. If one did take thought for himself, it was an indication that he was denying Christ. If the individual had not forsaken every aspect of his self, then he was not a part of the body or the Bride of Christ. One's only hope was to totally and completely empty self, and if thoughts of what one were doing or one's individuality came into the mind, the response should be, "Father, forgive me." Failure to do that was simply turning back to self-deification in the teachings of Trinity Foundation.

Trinity Foundation's interpretation of the apostle Paul's teaching on the vessel of wrath and the vessel of mercy was that the individual was either part of the Bride (vessel of mercy) or the whore (vessel of wrath). It did not matter whether you called yourself a believer. The proof of whether you were part of the Bride or part of the whore was your response to the stimuli in your environment. If you had not forsaken your thoughts, if you were not at complete peace, if you responded in any way to another person's criticism of you, if you did not see that every moment was perfect, if you wanted things to be different, if you did not see that everything around you was meaningless, then you were a vessel of wrath. It was that simple. Christ cannot occupy your vessel unless your vessel is empty of all self.

Your acceptance of your death is expressed by relinquishing all sense of control you have over your life and any direction it might take. You accept that you are dead and that your true life is only with Christ (see Col. 3:3). Ole used another scripture passage to expound on this doctrine: "If we deny *him* (Jesus), he also will deny us" (2 Tim. 2:12b). After quoting this verse, Ole would then interpret it by saying, "And we do not deny Jesus by saying that He does not exist. That's kindergarten stuff. We deny Jesus by saying that *we exist*." The point of this verse, according to Ole, is that you, as an individual human being, are dead; in other words, in Ole's teaching, the fact that the believer thinks he exists at all, is a lie of Satan.

The idea that you exist and have a life of your own is, therefore, an illusion, the great deception of the "antichrist." And who, by the way, is the antichrist? Ole taught that the antichrist was none other than your own mind, using 1 John 2:22: "Who is a liar but he that denieth that Jesus is the Christ? He is an antichrist, that denieth the Father and the Son." Ole would explain that the antichrist is actually one's mind, because it is the mind that thinks it is a separate being with a life of its own and, in doing so, denies Christ.

When Adam and Eve ate of the tree of the knowledge of good and evil, they died, and the whole human race died with them. Ole would often say that there are only two people who have ever lived, Adam and Christ. If it had not been for the coming of the second Adam (Jesus), there would have been no possibility for life at all. The members of the human race are not people with eternal spirits; they are simply manifestations of one of the two beings with such spirits, Adam and Jesus. Adam, when he fell, gave himself over to sin and became subject to Satan.

Ole would use the following metaphor illustrated by the parts of the human body to enlighten his disciples: No matter how much the thumb might think that it is a being—that it is alive, if it should become separate from the rest of the body, it would die. In like manner, you, as an individual person, are either a part of the body of Satan or you are a part of the body of Christ. The only thing that is of real importance is the body to which you are connected. It does not matter that you are a good person. If you are part of the body of Satan, part of the whole system that teaches self for self, then you will perish eternally.

The only enemy of faith is one's mind. One's mind is the antichrist according to Ole; therefore, since a person's mind is the antichrist, unless he lives in community, he cannot be freed from his bondage. The individual always wants things to change. The mind cannot possibly conceive that the state it is in is exactly as it should have been. Anytime you want conditions to change it means that you have not truly heard God. The individual has to come to that place where he loses the capacity to judge that every moment is not as it should have been. If one is not at peace, not content, if irritated at someone, or if worried about something, then he is not "in Christ" and is a vessel of wrath. Christ cannot occupy where self is, so the evidence that the individual is a vessel of wrath is the display of any self-seeking or mere thought for his needs or wants in any aspect. In the Trinity epistemology, the individual is never to consider self in any arena; one had to totally empty himself.

Ole taught that the only time a "child of hell" was defined in the Bible was in Genesis 3. The child of hell is one who judges for himself good and evil. There is only one who can judge good and evil and that is God. The renewing of one's mind, then, is the emptying of all thoughts, all judgments, feelings, and any perceptions associated with the senses. Christ cannot occupy where self is; therefore, you must empty your mind before God can take over. Because your thoughts are not His thoughts (Isaiah 55:8), your only hope is to take absolutely no thought for your own life. Your only hope is to completely and totally abandon all self-seeking.

What keeps you from emptying yourself and totally committing yourself to the body of Christ—the Trinity community—is of course, your mind, the antichrist. Your true personality, the expression of Christ Himself in your form, can only be found in the surrender of your identity and your individuality to God through the process of "laying down your life" in a community of believers. As long as you seek to have an existence apart from the church, you are walking in darkness and are separating yourself from the source of life.

Because the church of the last two thousand years had missed these fundamental truths and we at Trinity Foundation were the only ones teaching the "full counsel of God," to disunite from Trinity Foundation was to separate from the only possibility of a life in God. It was our mind that lied to us and said that we could have a life apart from God, a life of our own, a life apart from the body of Christ. The effect of this teaching was to produce a cult-induced phobia so that people felt that to leave the community was to leave God.

In many ways Ole discovered the perfect mind-control doctrine. An individual's capacity to think is undermined when told that his mind is the antichrist. If you can convince your followers to believe that their own minds are the enemy, then you have them absolutely in your power. The problem with telling a person that his mind is the antichrist is that there is no other medium for learning the facts about God other than through the mind. Indeed, every single act that is important to a believer—faith, repentance, joy, love, etc.—are all aspects of the mind. Therefore, what Ole's nonsense phrase, "your mind is the antichrist," comes to mean is your mind is the antichrist when it is thinking thoughts that question Ole Anthony. Of course, this was never stated overtly. Instead, Ole used the process of questioning and criticizing people who were doing nothing other than acting rationally in their own best interests. They were grilled on the point until they capitulated and confessed that they were committing some grievous sin by simply doing what any other reasonable person would have done in that situation.

Self-will can certainly be a problem for human beings, and learning to surrender and let go of our selfish desires is an essential component of both human and Christian growth; however, within the context of an authoritarian cult, when you disengage your will, you become exceedingly easy to manipulate. While Ole was, on the one hand, teaching his minions to surrender their will, abandon their false selves, and avenge themselves of their antichrist minds, on the other hand, he was continuing to wield extraordinary influence over their daily lives. Even though there was some spiritual truth in what he taught, his willingness to exploit the teaching for his own aggrandizement and for the control of others made it the perfect set-up for a cult.

Another of Ole's teachings was his doctrine that the believer never has to make a decision. Decisions are made when we use our minds—which, again, he considered to be the "antichrist"—to weigh evidence and make choices. However, Ole taught that nothing but corruption could possibly come from such a process. Instead, the believer should always wait on the clear direction of God, no matter how foolish it may seem to wait. God would lead by the process of the cloud, just as he led the children of Israel forth from Egypt by having them follow the cloud by day and the pillar of fire by night. Whenever the cloud was "down" or station-ary, the Israelites did not move from their resting place. In his excessively allegorical approach to interpreting the scriptures, Ole said that the cloud being "down" referred to any doubt that a person had in coming to a decision because God would always overtly and directly lead you. If an individual did not know what to do, he simply did not make any decisions.

Ole's definition of doubt was to halt between two options. If you thought there were two options or that there were two possible courses of action that you could take, then you had doubt by definition, and therefore, you had to wait until it became clear. God would eliminate one of the options and it would be obvious what you should do. Anytime you faced a decision, you were to simply wait until there was no doubt. Therefore, you never really had to make a decision. You only had to wait until one of the options was taken away. To further complicate a person's decision-making process, if Ole or the Bible study teachers had a concern or felt that that the member had "a cloud"—any doubt or uncertainty whatsoever—then that member should refuse to make any decision until there was complete peace.

The effect of this process was that it induced a state of extreme passivity in Ole's disciples, and they ultimately handed de facto control of their lives over to him. Of course, this control was exercised in the name of servant-hood. Ole would say that he was only trying to help people align their lives and actions with the will of God. In reality, it is often difficult to have total certainty with absolutely no doubt that you are making the right decision. Waiting for that certitude can paralyze your decision-making ability and make you easily influenced by strong-minded leaders such as Ole. A Christian writer once said that Satan would use a lake of truth to hide a pint of poison. In thinking back through what was taught at Trinity Foundation, I find this to be the case. At any given

Bible study, you were likely to hear things that certainly fit within the broad interpretation of orthodox Christian teaching. Ole taught and believed in the divinity of Christ, the substitutionary atonement, the Holy Trinity, a personal devil, and the authority of the scriptures. He also believed in the charismatic gifts in a way that, while not universal to the church, would not be considered strange in the Holiness and Pentecostal churches.

The fact is that some of what Ole said about these issues was not far off from what some of the strongest interpreters of Christian doctrine have said, including Augustine, Luther, and Calvin. In fact, one of the very few books Ole ever recommended to his followers to read was *Bondage of the Will*, by Martin Luther. The point of Luther's book was that man could do nothing to effect his own salvation because, as a fallen creature, his will was a manifestation of his sin nature. Ole absolutely would have agreed with that. It is only by completely letting go of his own will in total surrender to God that man can be a participant in Christ's salvation. Actually, Ole's doctrine was very Calvinistic, though I do not think Ole had read or studied much of Calvin. He nonetheless bought into Calvin's notion concerning the absolute depravity of man.

However, many of Ole's teachings fell outside of the mainstream church, and were ultimately heretical, especially his doctrine of the "high-place identities," which I explained in Chapter 6, "Breaking Spirits." In his introduction to *The Cruelty of Heresy: An Affirmation of Christian Orthodoxy*, C. FitzSimons Allison wrote, "If a teaching is wrong opinion rather than right opinion the consequences are cruel, the Christian faith is distorted, and people who follow these teachings are hurt." [1]

Would that Ole had understood this. Instead, his arrogance told him that he could reinterpret all of Christian theology and come up with a system that was more accurate and closer to the real gospel than anything anyone had done for the last two thousand years. The effect of this was two-fold: Primarily, it excused him for his lack of a formal theological education. It was easy for him to make patronizing and dismissive comments about important Christian thinkers like Augustine, Thomas Aquinas, John Calvin, Soren Kierkegaard, Rudolf Bultmann, or Karl Barth because he had never studied their work nor struggled with their ideas in a meaningful way; secondly, it had the subtle effect of placing him on a level with Christ's disciples. He even overtly said that his role was the same as the apostle Paul's, and he often referred to himself as an apostle. Ole seemed to believe that he was bringing the mysteries of God into a time and culture where they were not already known, just as the original twelve apostles had taken the gospel of Christ into the pagan world that surrounded them in the first century.

"The gospel of Christ is not good news! It's bad news!" Ole often proclaimed to his disciples as discussed earlier in chapter six. And it was bad news for those of us who became involved with Trinity Foundation. The word gospel in the Greek language actually means "good news" or a "good message," but Ole insisted that the gospel was bad news because it cost the individual everything—his life, his right to his own thoughts, opinions, and his very possessions. In reality, it was Trinity Foundation that cost us everything.

CHAPTER 9

I Can't Hear God Anymore

Early in our dating relationship, Doug had explained to me how weddings were conducted at the Trinity Foundation and that the group had to approve of the union before a marriage could be sanctioned. I recall thinking that the practice sounded strange, but I believed that my ability to choose a marriage partner was defective. Since my previous attempts at marriage had not been successful, I felt a sense of security in knowing that when and if I married again, it would be with the undeniable certainty that God ordained it, as evidenced by the blessing of the Trinity Foundation. Not only was I willing to set up the group, along with its leader, to be my mediator with God, but I also longed to have what I perceived was a truly spiritual wedding.

My first and only observance of a wedding at the Trinity Foundation occurred during the first year that I was part of the group. Weddings were not frequent occurrences. In fact, there had been only one wedding during the seven years I was there, and I had to admit that it seemed very mystical and spiritual.

The wedding ceremony was a sacred event at the Trinity Foundation because marriage symbolized Christ and His Bride, the church. Weddings were communal events and were for the edification of the entire church body. Since the wedding and the marriage were for the group as a whole, and not just—or even primarily—for the individuals who were being married, the leaders of the group had control over most every aspect of the wedding, including whether or not there could even be a wedding.

The only time of the year that the Trinity Foundation considered appropriate for weddings was during the Feast of Tabernacles, which was observed in the fall. Ole taught that it was only during this event that the engaged couple and everyone else could see the full picture of marriage that God had ordained.

The civil wedding took place first and was presided over by the only ordained minister in the Trinity Foundation. From Trinity Foundation's viewpoint, the civil wedding was only a formality. Its purpose was to allow the family and friends of the couple from outside the group to be a part of the celebration, but it was only a social custom and not the true marriage ceremony. The true wedding, the Trinity Foundation ceremony, would take place seven days later.

The civil wedding would be followed by seven days of celebrations and parties with the whole community involved in the celebration of the betrothal. The couple began living together after the first wedding, but were forbidden to consummate the marriage. To ensure that they were not tempted to engage in sexual activity, children of Trinity Foundation members would take turns spending the night with the newlyweds.

On the night before the spiritual wedding, the community would meet for a ceremony to "smash the paradise apple." The purpose of this ceremony would be to expose the fallacy of one's judgment regarding what was good and what was evil.

Ole taught that it was God—and God alone—who could distinguish between good and evil—not man. Attempting to distinguish good from evil was to put oneself in the category of the omniscient God. The individual with only a finite mind could never understand God, and since the person's mind was the antichrist, it could not be trusted. The individual's only task was to trust God and to understand that everything was perfect. Trusting God and understanding that any situation was perfect required the destruction of one's judgments and personal opinions about how things should be. Only by abandoning one's own thoughts could the individual be completely dependent upon God.

At some point in the ceremony, each individual would take a pomegranate (symbolizing the paradise apple) and hurl it against an altar that had been constructed for that purpose. The pomegranate represented all of a person's ideas, opinions, and judgments and thus, when the fruit was smashed against the altar, the individual was then free from all self and ready to live truly in the moment, trusting only God.

During the week prior to the spiritual wedding and the celebration of the Feast of Tabernacles, a representative from each of the Bible study groups would spend a night in a "booth." Using branches and sticks, members of the Trinity Foundation would build a dwelling big enough for two or three adults. The booth would symbolize the transient nature of man's earthly journey as "strangers and pilgrims" on this earth. This life on Earth was not our "home." Our final destination was to be with God. On the same night that we smashed the pomegranate, we would also take a branch from the booth and burn it in the fire signifying our desire to leave this world and join in the marriage supper that God had prepared for us.

The day of a Trinity Foundation wedding was always filled with joy and excitement. Everyone was caught up in the allegory and worked all day setting up a huge tent, which was laboriously transformed into a representation of the temple. White linen and fine netting of rayon or nylon draped the walls and tables, bathing the makeshift temple in pure white. Candles were strategically suspended around the tent to produce a subtle and sensuous ambience. Hundreds of beautiful white flowers adorned the walls and tables, which were set up for the evening dinner. It was a magical backdrop for the wedding ceremony and the Feast of Tabernacles.

Towards the evening, the women gathered at the bride's house to help her dress and prepare for the ceremony. After the veil was placed on her head, her attendants, amidst singing and laughter, escorted her down the street to the tent site. At the same time, the groom was assisted by the men in the group and was led out by his attendants. Everyone was dressed in white, symbolizing the wedding garment—the righteousness of Christ.

Before the processional, when the members began the journey up the candlelit pathway to the transformed sanctuary, Ole would stand above the people on the front porch and further set the stage for this magical evening. He would remind his followers that, as we walked up the pathway to the temple (i.e., the tent), each step that we took symbolized our passage from flesh to spirit—from isolated individuals to members of the Bride of Christ. He reminded us that the white garments we wore meant that we had put on the righteousness of God. Finally, with great fanfare, Ole pronounced that the gate was closed, and all who were outside the gate were lost. We, however, were the fortunate ones, as we were the Trinity Foundation and inside the gate. We then proceeded up the candlelit pathway into an evening of joy as we entered the "New Jerusalem."

I longed to have a wedding celebration that was a spiritual expression of my commitment to God and my husband.

Doug and I had sought approval to be married numerous times from Ole and the elders; however, in their wisdom, the time had not arrived. I had trusted Ole's discernment of God's will in his position on our marriage. I trusted that he and the elders only wanted what was best for Doug and me. My trust, nevertheless, broke down in the fall of 1999 when another couple, David and Ginger received approval to be married at the next Feast of Tabernacles in 2000. This couple was much younger than Doug and me. They were in their twenties, while we were in our forties. Additionally, they had been dating only three years as opposed to our seven. I remember feeling such a sense of disappointment that they were given the next opportunity, because it meant that we could not be married for at least two more years. I also had feelings of guilt because I did not feel joyful upon receiving the news of their wedding announcement.

The sanction of David and Ginger's wedding was the beginning of the crack in my wall of denial that I was involved in an excessively controlling group. Another fissure in that wall surfaced during a dinner party I held for Doug and two couples who were also members of the community.

At one point during the evening someone said, "You guys sure have been dating a long time! Are you ever going to get married?" I flippantly answered, "The Trinity won't let us," to which one of the women replied, "That's a bunch of bullshit!" Another guest responded, "What do you mean the Trinity won't let you? I'm a part of Trinity, and I didn't know it was even up for consideration!"

One of the cardinal, though unspoken, rules of the Trinity Foundation was that it was forbidden to speak critically of Ole or the elders, so the discussion was promptly abandoned. Those comments, however, gnawed at my mind. I saw that the real opposition to our marriage was not the community, but rather it was Ole and the two elders who were my Bible study teachers. I also thought it was ironic, perhaps even hypocritical, that the young woman who had recently secured the approval to get married was the daughter of my Bible study teachers, Jan and Garth Brown.

These two events also penetrated Doug's denial. One day as he returned from a doctor's appointment, he drove by Highland Park Presbyterian Church and decided to stop. He had been thinking more and more about marrying me and felt in his heart that the time was right, yet every time he discussed the matter with Ole or one of the elders, he was admonished to wait on God to make it clear that the marriage was His will.

"I sensed that there was a problem, and I needed to talk about it," said Doug. "I wanted to know if I was getting good advice. Something was not right, and I needed to consult with someone other than a member of the Trinity Foundation. There was no one I could talk to in the group's leadership because all of the elders took their cues from Ole and could only parrot whatever opinion Ole was espousing. I walked in the front door of Highland Park Presbyterian Church's office and said, 'I am having a spiritual crisis, and I need to speak to a minister.'"

The receptionist directed him to the church's counseling center where he made an appointment with a therapist, Debbie Devine, who specialized in dealing with abuse victims. When he returned for his appointment the next day, Doug explained his situation and said that he felt he had given too much control over his life to his religious leaders—Ole, in particular. In the process of the counseling session, Debbie said, "I don't hear you having doubts about marrying Wendy. I hear doubts about your church's leadership."

"The therapist's response was powerful because it validated that there was another point of view besides that of the Trinity Foundation," said Doug. "At some point during my counseling session with Debbie, I said something to the effect that, for me, God did not really exist outside of the group. The therapist allowed me to finish my train of thought before backing me up to say, 'Did you hear what you just said—that God doesn't exist outside of the group?' A part of me had always realized that it was absurd to think that God was contained in this little group in east Dallas. I realized how small I had made God seem. When Debbie said that, a seed was planted and I began to think critically again. Although it would still be several months until I finally left Trinity Foundation, I think the process started when I saw that no group—especially not one consisting of just a few dozen people in east Dallas—could have a monopoly on God," Doug recalled.

My own awakening came shortly after that, on that fateful spring day when I had my confrontation with Ole. During the seven years I had been dating Doug, Ole had continued to express his disapproval of our desire to marry, but, for some reason, on that morning, I had to confront him. I had had previous minor disagreements with Ole. Once—and only once—when I first started attending the group I asked Ole for a copy of Trinity Foundation's financial statement. He became angry with me and rebuked me for my lack of trust. I did not make that mistake again, but that was nothing compared to the confrontation I had with Ole that day in March. That day I had an unprecedented clash with Ole over his use of scripture to justify his position that Doug and I were not ready to marry.

I had been a member of the Trinity Foundation for seven years. I knew that a true believer was always to be at peace and that everything was always perfect. According to the doctrine of the Trinity Foundation, if you thought anything should change, you were not at peace. Not being at peace was proof that you had crucified Christ afresh and had resurrected self. Self was resurrected every time that one thought that something should be different than it was. Self raised its ugly head every time one thought of his own needs. We were not to consider our evil self and its desires. I was clearly not at peace or "at rest" in the vernacular of the Trinity Foundation.

My confrontation with Ole Anthony that spring day produced an overwhelming fear that I was about to lose everything that was precious to me — my community, my new family, my sense of purpose, and my relationship with Doug. I believed that Doug was far more committed to Ole and the Trinity Foundation than he was to me or our relationship. I had committed the inexcusable sin of challenging the leader of Trinity Foundation. And yet, I could not let Ole continue to use his position of authority to distort God's Word.

I snapped. Or rather, I snapped back. I snapped back to the person I was before I joined the Trinity Foundation. I snapped back and realized that I had somehow become a part of a spiritually abusive and ultra-authoritarian religious group. "I can't hear God's voice anymore!" I had shouted at Ole. "Your voice has gotten too loud!" I snapped, and in that single moment, I began to slowly find my way back to God.

CHAPTER 10

A Wedding Without a Blessing

After my verbal altercation with Ole, Doug had gone to the Trinity Foundation's office to wait his turn with Ole. Doug knew that after Ole had finished eating his breakfast, he would be called into a meeting with Ole over what I had done. As Doug was fearfully waiting for Ole, it dawned on him that he didn't have to subject himself to the barrage of condemnation from Ole, which was sure to happen. Without saying a word to anyone, he left and drove off in one of the foundation's vehicles.

In all the years that Doug had been a member of the Trinity Foundation, he had never committed such a flagrant act of defiance. But, as he recalled, "It was like a revelation came over me that I didn't have to submit to another one of Ole's tirades. I didn't have to meet with him and listen to his browbeating." Doug left and drove around for a while trying to decide what to do. He eventually went to his father's house and told him what had happened. Welcoming his prodigal son back, his father offered to let him stay there until Doug decided what to do and provided him with some clothes since Doug had left without anything.

After work that evening, I met Doug and his father, Gordon, at a Mexican restaurant. I had never talked with Gordon about the Trinity Foundation and did not realize until that evening how strongly both of Doug's parents felt about Ole and the group. Doug's mother died the summer before we met so I had never had the pleasure of knowing her. From what I had learned about her personality, she was an introverted, quiet, intelligent woman who loved to read. Although Doug had alluded to the fact that his mother was never happy about his involvement with Ole, that evening, Gordon explained that Doris hated Ole with a passion from the first moment she met him. On two or three occasions, this shy, reserved woman felt so strongly that Trinity Foundation was a negative influence in her son's life that she had confrontational meetings with Ole. From the time Doug became involved with the group until her death in 1992, Doris had held a deep fear that her son was involved with something almost demonic. Gordon had also had concerns, but was not as vocal as his wife had been in discussing them.

Over dinner at the restaurant, we discussed Doug's relationship with Ole, which Doug was now describing as "unhealthy." Doug decided that he needed to get away for a while so that he could think. Earlier that day, Doug called his old college roommate, Marty, who had been a member of the Trinity Foundation but who had left several years before. Doug had not had much contact with him because there was an unspoken rule at Trinity Foundation about friendships with former members. Marty invited Doug to come stay with him for a few days, and Doug accepted the invitation.

Later that evening before I left to return home, Doug officially proposed. Since we had both been married before, we decided to have a simple ceremony performed by a justice of the peace.

"Will you be OK on the block until I get back? I hate leaving you there alone," Doug asked before I left.

"Of course, I will. Why wouldn't I be?" I had no idea what he was talking about, but in the days to come I would look back on his question and understand his concern.

I drove the Trinity Foundation vehicle back to the block, and, upon my return, I saw Allan and Frank and told them that Doug and I planned to marry the next week. Both of them hugged me and Allan said, "It's about time, though you caused quite a stir in the community. Everyone is pretty angry with you and Doug."

The next morning, Saturday, as I was walking my dog, I saw one of my Bible study leaders and told him about our plans to get married. Garth was visibly upset, but his only words were, "Are you sure that's what you should do?"

"Of course I am," I replied. "Doug and I have known each other for seven years and we have been waiting to get married. We had wanted to get married at Trinity but …" There was no need to repeat the same arguments we had been through so many times before.

The tension during this brief conversation with Garth left me wondering if I would be permitted to come to Purim later that day. Purim was one of the Jewish feasts that the Trinity Foundation observed each year. It had been described as a type of Jewish Mardi Gras and was an event we all looked forward to. The day of Purim began with a fast, a "wimp" fast as Ole defined it, which began at sunrise and only lasted till late afternoon. The fast was considered a minor fast because you only had to abstain from food and cigarettes, whereas with some of the other fasts you could not have anything to drink, including water. The fast commemorated Esther when she abstained from food for three days in preparation for her appointment with Ahasuerus, King of Persia.

The book of Esther contains the story of Purim. Esther was a beautiful young woman who was chosen to come to the king's palace to be a part of his harem. The king fell in love with her and after his first queen refused to submit to him, King Ahasuerus crowned Esther as his queen. Esther had been raised by her cousin, Mordecai, and was a Jewish woman; however, King Ahasuerus was not aware of her nationality. The other main character in the book of Esther was Haman—Haman was the villain, the evil one. He was the highest official in the King's Court and enjoyed his status so much that he required all of the common people to bow before him. Esther's uncle, Mordecai, refused to bow to him, which infuriated Haman and as a result, Haman plotted to annihilate all of the Jewish people living in Persia.

Mordecai became aware of this plot by Haman and informed Esther. He pleaded with her to talk with the King and convince him not to kill the Jewish people. Esther reminded her uncle that it was against the law for anyone to go to the King without being summoned by him. Mordecai, though, was convinced that she had been preordained for this purpose and in his words recorded in the book of Esther, "And who knows whether you have not come to the kingdom for such a time as this?" (Esther 4:14b, RSV).

Esther agreed to go to the King, even though she could be put to death for disobeying the law. In a verse familiar to most Christians, Esther replied, "If I perish, I perish." (Esther 4:16b). She, therefore, approached the King with a plan to turn the table on Haman. At the end of the story Haman, the enemy, was put to death and Mordecai was honored.

The purpose of observing Purim as explained by Ole was to reflect upon how we judge good and evil for ourselves. Each of the Bible study groups met around two o'clock in the afternoon to discuss the purpose of Purim and read aloud the assigned scriptures from Exodus and other Old Testament verses centered upon the Amalekites, which Ole taught represented the individual "after the flesh," the aspect of mankind that God hated. Haman, the villain in the book of Esther, was an Amalekite. After several hours of discussion and reading of scripture, the fast would be broken with a glass of wine and usually fruit or cheese.

Then the fun part began. People took turns reading aloud from the book of Esther, and each time the name Esther was mentioned we took a sip of red wine and toasted Esther, the "type" of the Bride. When Mordecai's name was mentioned we clapped and cheered, but when Haman's name was read we booed, hissed, and stomped our feet in protest. Ole taught that you should drink sufficiently so that you become confused about when to curse Haman and when to bless Mordecai. Since Esther's name was mentioned approximately seventy times in the book and we began sipping wine on relatively empty stomachs since we had only broken the fast with a small amount of food, it usually did not take long for people to start confusing Haman and Mordecai. By the time that Esther's name had been read five or six times, members were beginning to feel the effects of the wine. And certainly by the time the whole book of Esther had been read — which usually lasted two or more hours — it was not uncommon for everyone to be intoxicated.

Around the time Purim was to begin, I went out into my front yard and saw Susan crossing the street. Susan lived across the street from me in one of the condominiums that Trinity Foundation managed. When I was working for Dallas County Mental Health and Mental Retardation (administering a mental health outpatient program for offenders with mental illness), I had hired Susan as the intake worker. She was an excellent staff person and I had thoroughly enjoyed working with her. After she had worked in the program for about two years, she resigned to take a job elsewhere. I had spoken frequently of the Trinity Foundation during her employment and, after her resignation, she wrote me a letter asking me to invite her to one of the Bible studies. From the first time that she attended, she had become a loyal follower of Ole's.

When Susan saw me, she stopped to talk and asked me if I was coming to Purim. I told her that Doug and I were planning to get married and I did not know if it was permissible for me to come to Purim. "Of course you are supposed to come. When I get over to Garth's, I'll make sure—and then give you a call."

Thirty minutes went by—and then an hour. The phone did not ring. I knew that they would have to discuss my situation, but it seemed like it was taking an extremely long time. I kept waiting for the phone to ring, signaling that I was still considered a part of the group, but the phone never rang. Three o'clock came and went—then four o'clock and five o'clock. By six o'clock, I felt like a little girl whose friends had all gone to the birthday party and I was the only one who had not been invited. I left my house to get something to eat and when I returned, the phone finally rang. It was Garth, one of my Bible study leaders. "What are you doing?" he asked.

"Just waiting to see if y'all would call me," I replied.

"Well, why don't you come on down?"

My Bible study leaders lived in another of the two-story duplexes on the block—three houses down from mine. My spirit lifted after he called and I hurriedly walked down the street to their house. I was not prepared for the angry mob—their emotions heightened from all the wine—that awaited me.

"So what's this about you and Doug getting married?" one of them demanded.

"Doug and I decided to go ahead and get married—we're going to go to a justice of the peace next week," I explained.

"Where is Doug?" another person demanded.

"He went to Memphis to visit Marty for a few days." I should have known that would not go over well. Marty was a defector—a former member who had left the group eight or nine years earlier.

"Please don't do this, Wendy," Ginger begged, starting to cry.

"Ginger, we love each other and we've been dating longer than you and David. We're sure we are ready to marry, and we don't see any reason to continue waiting."

In reply, another member asked, "It doesn't matter that your Bible study group and the elders don't agree? We don't have God's peace about this. You are making a terrible decision."

"Why? Why is this such a terrible decision? Doug will continue to be a Levite. We will just be together. My job is going well; everything is all right with his kids." All the past arguments against our marriage were no longer valid. My job was stable. I had purchased a house on the block, which I thought indicated a high level of commitment to the group. Doug's kids were doing fine.

At that moment, Stan came over to me, stuck his face right in mine, and started screaming obscenities at me. I backed away—the attack became more vicious. I was shocked. Why in the world were these people—people I considered my family—screaming at me and cursing me? I realized that they were all drunk, but it did not make any sense. Why were they all so angry about Doug and me getting married? I could not figure it out.

Wanting desperately to leave, but knowing the Trinity rule about not leaving during confrontations, I sat through an incredibly brutal verbal attack. Apparently, there was no way I would be able to appease their anger. Finally, claiming to be exhausted, I left.

When I got home, I called Doug to tell him of my experience. "I was afraid something like that would happen," he said. "Just hang in there until I get back."

The next day, Sunday, I sent an e-mail to my friends and family to let them know about our plans to marry.

Dear Friends and Family,

Doug and I have decided to marry this Thursday. Unfortunately, we have been unable to secure the blessing of Ole, and it has caused no small stir. I exploded at Ole on Friday after I felt he was trying to manipulate Doug using scripture and the cross. It was more than I could take. I don't think I have ever been so angry in all my life nor gone off on someone as much.

Well, Doug left to clear his head and get some distance so he could rethink his relationship to Ole and the group. This is, as you can image, a biggie. He has known Ole for over twenty years and has given his life to the work of the foundation. Ole has been his surrogate father and spiritual mentor, but we both feel that we need to take some control back, or we have become nothing but cult members.

Please pray for us. It is an emotionally trying time. Some of the group members are having an extremely difficult time with this. It's almost as if we have threatened their very belief system and security.

We love the church, even with all of its fallibilities. We would like it to be perfect and never disappoint, but it is made up of people like us who screw up a thousand times a day. We are still committed to the mission and vision of the Trinity Foundation and committed to abiding here through the good times and bad. Hopefully, this bad time will be over quickly.

Our plan now is to do the justice of the peace thing on Thursday. We are still very open to however God works this one out and to postpone if He should lead.

Send prayers.

Much love,
Wendy

I was delighted when I received numerous replies from individuals whom I knew that I had neglected since becoming a member of the Trinity Foundation. Their sweet messages affirmed that we were making the right decision:

Wendy,

Wow! I think I need to say it again … Wow! What a bittersweet time this must be for you. For what it's worth, ya'll have had my blessing for years! I'll certainly pray for God's grace to shine upon your marriage as well as to heal the emotional wounds with your church. I want to see you both, sometime soon.

Daralynn

Oh my dear Wendy and Doug: I will definitely pray for you at this time. Please let Steve and me know what else we can do to help. I love you and will be thinking of you on Thursday.

Your friend,
Melody

WOW, Wendy !!!

Sorry, I'm just now responding. I've been out of town and just now read my e-mail. I will pray for you and Doug and I am very happy for you. I'm glad that you all are making your decisions based on what God wants for you, because ultimately He is the only one whose approval counts.

Love,
Arlene

Dear Wendy (I'm copying Faith on this, too)

You go, girl! I'd wondered about why you and Doug hadn't married yet. Now I know.

I very much support you and Doug in your decision to stand accountable to God for this marriage, rather than to Ole. I know you'd like to have his blessing, but I think the Lord's blessing will make up for it!!

Grace, courage, wisdom and abundant love to you and Doug!

In Him,
Mary

Wender, I am so pleased that you and Doug are deciding to get married and am sad to hear that you are having another negative experience with a church body. Since our churches are made up of people who are fallible, we do tend to do many things wrong. But I know that the church fellowship should be a place of healing, support, encouragement, and a sharpening tool in God's hands to make us more like him. Don't despair about Christ's church, but maybe you need to look closely to see if this group with such a leader is acting in accordance with biblical principles. Our allegiance is not to a leader, charismatic, authoritarian, or otherwise, but to the Lord Jesus Christ.

I agree with Mary that, although you would like to have the blessing of Ole, it is far more important to have the Lord's blessing. If you have that, all else pales. You are right, Wender, that you should not follow a human being blindly, or you risk being a cult follower instead of a believer who can seek God's will through the Bible and in prayer.

Ultimately, you and Doug are responsible to God for your decisions and it is unfortunate that Ole feels that he has a place in dictating or sanctioning your choices. I will be in prayer for you that the Lord will lead you and that you will follow His direction.

Blessings on you,
Faith

On Monday I received an e-mail from one of the elders regarding our marriage plans. He had said that his son who was attending an out-of-state school was confused about what was going on with Doug and me. Without realizing that the e-mail I sent could be taken in a negative light, I forwarded his son the e-mail that I sent out to my friends and family. In my naiveté I also failed to realize that my e-mail would be circulated among all of the Trinity Foundation members who would become incensed when they saw the word *cult* in my message.

Our weekday Bible study meetings were held on Tuesday and Thursday evenings, and even though I was still somewhat traumatized by the response of my group on Purim, I headed down to my Bible study teachers' house on Tuesday evening. Ole, who was the teacher for the group called "Bananas," was not there that evening, so my Bible study group was meeting with the Bananas group. When I walked in a little late, Jan, one of my Bible study leaders, was reading the e-mail that I had written. She seemed surprised to see me and said, "I didn't know that you were coming tonight."

My response was, "It's Tuesday night — isn't that when we usually meet for Bible study?" Even with everything that had happened in the preceding days, I still thought that I was a part of the group.

Jan then handed me the e-mail that I had sent out and told me to read it aloud for the group. Apparently, it had been offensive to everyone at Trinity who had read it and they focused primarily upon the statement I made about it being a cult.

I tried to explain that I had not said Trinity was a cult, but that if Doug and I allowed others to control us, we had become cult members. I thought it was clear that I had placed the emphasis and the accountability, as well as the responsibility, on Doug and me rather than the group. But that was not their perception of my statements.

After I read the e-mail I sent out, people bombarded me with their thoughts and opinions. I reminded them of the statement in the e-mail I had written, "We are still committed to the mission and vision of the Trinity Foundation and committed to abiding here through the good times and bad. Hopefully, this bad time will be over quickly."

It did not seem to have an impact upon them. Their focal point still centered on the word cult and my statement that their belief system had been threatened. It was an extremely uncomfortable time. When you are the center of attention and everyone is angry with you, it can be very intimidating.

Other times when I had been on the "hot seat" there was an element of truth to whatever the group said to me: I was acting like a victim; or I was being rebellious; or I had trust issues, or whatever. But this time it was baffling, because I honestly could not understand why people would think that Doug and I were doing anything wrong. And Ole had said he "didn't give a rat's ass" if we got married, so why was everybody so upset about it? It was too weird. But, as was true in many instances, Trinity's stated doctrine was not consistent with its actions.

At what had to be the cruelest and most sadistic peak of the evening, Jan said to me, "If you marry Doug, God is going to kick your butt!"

I remember looking at her and thinking what a horrible, horrible thing to say to someone whose only sin at that moment was a desire to marry.

The day that Doug and I got married, her words played in my mind all day. On an intellectual level, I knew that what she had said was not true, but somewhere deep inside of me her words raised a tremendous sense of anxiety and fear. Driving to the justice of the peace, I was scared that something would happen to Doug on his way to our marriage ceremony—that he would be killed in a car wreck or something almost as disastrous.

In fact, all week long I had been waiting for God to "kick my butt." By this time in my Trinity experience I had come to see God as an angry, wrathful god. My perception of God had changed in the years I had been a part of the Trinity Foundation, and He had ceased to be the loving, caring God that I had first come to know. So, part of me feared that Jan was right, and during the week leading up to our wedding day, I was worried that something terrible would happen. Either something horrible would happen to Doug or he would change his mind.

The week before we married was undoubtedly one of the worst times in my life. I felt so alone and scared, and I had no one to talk with about my fears and my confusion. During the time that I was a member of the Trinity Foundation, I had emotionally distanced myself from my family and my friends. There were times when they would ask me questions about the Trinity Foundation and try to challenge some of my new beliefs, but I always dismissed their concerns. They were outsiders and could not possibly understand the revelations of God's mysteries that we at Trinity Foundation had been given. I always portrayed Trinity Foundation in a positive light. Never did I mention any problems or doubts. Never did I voice any critical remarks about the leader or my elders. Never did I divulge any of the family secrets. Even after I left the Trinity Foundation I was unable to talk to my old friends and family about the group. I did not have the words at that time to articulate the experience. Not only did I not have the words to explain what it was like, but I had an overpowering feeling of shame. After I began writing this book, one of my sisters commented that cults were like dysfunctional families. In dysfunctional families, there were unspoken rules about talking critically about one's family to others or about divulging the family secrets.

With all the emotional turmoil during the week before we married, even though we had waited such a long time to get married, we made few plans. The few people who were invited were called either the evening before or the morning before our afternoon ceremony.

Even so, the day was perfect. Two of my friends, Amanda and Katherine, came over to my house with a bouquet of flowers and a bottle of champagne. Doug's middle daughter, Melinda, who lived in Florida at the time, was in Dallas for the weekend, so she attended. My oldest sister and her husband and one of my nieces, Courtney, came. Doug's friend, Mark, served as the best man, and my good friend, Beryl, was my maid of honor. Doug's family had a dinner party awaiting us afterwards at the Olive Garden, where we had our own enclave to celebrate our marriage. Later, we spent the night at the Sheraton Hotel and made love for the first time.

The next day, Saturday, we drove to a couple's house in Austin, where a group of my friends had gathered and where we had another celebration of our marriage. The celebratory joyous spirit of our real friends and family made such a sharp contrast to the attitude of our Trinity "family."

During the week before Doug and I married, he had spent a few days with Marty, and when he came back to Dallas, he stayed with his dad again and then with Mark. The short time away from the group gave Doug an opportunity to think, which subsequently gave rise to doubts about the spiritual health of the community. Doug and I discussed our continued involvement with the group, and although we had begun to see some of the problems, neither of us were at the point where we were ready to leave. We were still committed to the mission of the Trinity Foundation, and even though we had been hurt by the reaction of the members over our marriage, we still loved them and wanted to continue to be a part of the group.

In his many hours of discussions with Mark, Doug asked him if he thought we should leave Trinity. Mark replied that was a decision Doug and I would have to make for ourselves. "I will support you either way," he said. "If you decide to go back, though, my hope is that you will be able to change the culture." In our naiveté, Doug and I thought we could do that, and after our marriage and brief weekend trip to Austin, we returned to the block on a Sunday afternoon, planning to go to Seder. The day before we married, I received an e-mail from one of the elders, Luke, who indicated that Ole had met with the elders and wanted to let us know that they loved us and we were still considered a part of the community. Luke was one of the few people in the group who seemed supportive, but his take on the discussion must have been skewed. Either that or it was another example of the conflict between what Trinity Foundation said and what they did.

When we returned, Doug called Garth to let him know we were back and were planning to come to Seder. Garth's response was of a very different spirit than Luke's: "I don't think that's a good idea. You and Wendy need to meet with the elders before fellowship can be restored." Obviously, there were still negative emotions over our marriage.

Rather than grace, openness, forgiveness, and a welcoming spirit, Doug felt that Garth was telling him that he needed to see the enormity of what he had done — that he needed to recognize how bad and wrong he was. That evening was difficult for both of us. Sunday evenings were always spent in Seder, and now we had been told that we were not welcome. A sense of sadness and confusion permeated our first evening on the block as a married couple.

The next night, Monday, we met with the elders. The stated reason that we had not been allowed to go to Seder was because Doug needed to explain his actions regarding leaving the block without telling anyone and "deserting the Oklahoma group," a new Bible study group that had been started in Oklahoma. Doug had been scheduled to lead Purim for this group. Although we knew that the source of the conflict was our rebellion against Ole's authority by marrying, the purported problem became about Doug leaving the Oklahoma group as well as his own Bible study group "uncovered." The fact that other elders were available to take Doug's place in Oklahoma and that he shared leadership responsibilities with Garth and Jan for their combined Bible study group did not appear to be relevant.

Ole told Doug that he needed to acknowledge what an enormous thing he had done by separating from the group and leaving them alone—and that he must repent. "Unless you acknowledge your sin and ask for repentance, fellowship cannot be restored, Doug."

Doug replied, "Ole, in the letter I wrote you last week before Wendy and I got married, I asked you to forgive me for not calling you, and for communicating in writing instead. I was feeling very vulnerable and didn't feel that I was ready to talk to you. In the past, you have always said negative things when I've talked about wanting to marry Wendy, and I always backed down. I realize now that my communication with you has been very ineffective for many reasons, most of them my fault. Nevertheless, let me state unequivocally, that being married to Wendy is what I wanted to do, and I am sorry for the ways that this is hurting you and others. I was not trying to hurt anyone. I just reached a point that I felt like I was being completely stonewalled on this. If I didn't do something, I was going to end up living in total resentment."

"Doug, you can't honestly think that you can waltz back in here without having to account for your actions. You are an elder and a Levite and a Bible study teacher. You left your group uncovered. Your group members had nowhere to turn if they encountered problems during the week you were gone."

"I understand that, Ole, and doubtless, I could have done some things differently, but I needed some time to think through my decisions, and I knew that if I had talked with you, you would have convinced me not to marry Wendy. I understand that it was problematic for me to leave the block for a week, but I needed to sort out some things and I didn't know of any other way to do it. I certainly realize that there are people with some hurt feelings that Wendy and I will have to talk things through with, but I was hoping that the elders would take the approach that Luke's e-mail indicated, which is that there can be reconciliation and renewed fellowship."

The discussion went on and on. Ole and the elders needed Doug to grovel and to weep and cry and plead to be allowed back in the group. Doug's reaction was not what they wanted.

At one point, I became so angry at their attack on Doug that I had to go outside and regroup. Since leaving is analogous to murdering in the Trinity world, as I got up, I explained that I was only leaving for a few minutes to get some fresh air. While sitting on the steps of the front porch, I saw Jake who lived next door. When he saw that I was crying he came over and gave me a hug and tried to assure me that things were going to work out. "They are just hurt that Doug left without talking it over with them first and that y'all went ahead and got married without their blessing. Just apologize and everything will be fine."

When I returned, Ole had decided that he needed to talk with the elders privately about our situation. We were told to come back on Wednesday evening to meet again. During the next meeting, we were informed that Doug's punishment would be the removal of his status as an elder and Bible study teacher at least until Tabernacles, which was six months away.

Doug maintained hope for months after we married that Trinity would eventually accept our relationship. Doug idealistically believed that at some point the marriage would be embraced. He even had a fantasy about a Trinity celebration or, at the least, a toast. "I think one night during Big Group they are going to surprise us with maybe a little reception with cake and champagne—or maybe just a toast," Doug said. "You'll see, Wendy, they will come around at some point and be happy for us, and when they do, it will be very special. It will happen, Wendy. We just need to be patient."

It never happened. In fact, it was more often ignored. Throughout the next six months, there were several times when Ole would talk about marriage and list some of the married couples. Doug and I were never included. We realized that it had been a sensitive issue, so we felt that it was best just to give them some time to work through their emotions.

The summer after we married, we went to Pentecost, another of the Jewish feasts that the group observed. Pentecost was the second of the three big annual pilgrimage feasts where the Jewish people, and now, the Trinity people, were required to present themselves to God or they would be separated from the promise. The pilgrimage feasts all represented an increasing awareness and understanding of the mysteries of God. Pentecost revealed the mystery of the power given to the Bride of Christ.

Trinity's celebration of Pentecost was held at a Christian camp near Lake Whitney in Texas each year around Memorial Day, and we would spend the entire weekend there. It was a fun getaway with free time to enjoy swimming, volleyball, and shopping in the nearby outlet stores. And there was no fasting associated with Pentecost, which everyone appreciated.

Two things happened that summer at Pentecost that signaled to us that our marriage was still an issue with Trinity. One was that we were not assigned to the married couples' cabin, and the other was conveyed in one of the Trinity customs at Pentecost. Each year during Pentecost there was a ceremony in which all the members were rebaptized in the camp's swimming pool. The married couples were always baptized together because they were "one flesh." Over the years, I had watched the married couples get baptized together during Pentecost and thought how wonderful it would be when Doug and I could be baptized together. The summer after we married I could hardly wait until Pentecost. Ole, however, decided for the first time since the practice was initiated, that the couples should be baptized separately—another covert message that our marriage was still not acceptable.

After Doug and I were married, I tried to reintegrate into the community, but I was beginning to have doubts about the true nature of the group. During the week before we were married, Doug spent several days with his friends, Marty and Mark, who were both former members. During the long talks he had with each of these men, some of the truth of the reality of Trinity Foundation seeped into his understanding. Mark mentioned several books that he had read after leaving the group. During a trip to Austin the summer after we married, we obtained copies of some of the cult literature Mark had recommended and I read segments of these books out loud as Doug drove.

One of the books in particular, *Toxic Faith*, by Stephen Arterburn and Jack Felton, was instrumental in increasing our awareness of the problems with Trinity Foundation. The authors give a definition of toxic-faith as "a destructive and dangerous involvement in a religion that allows the religion, not a relationship with God, to control a person's life … a defective faith with an incomplete or tainted view of God …"[1] The chapter in the book that disturbed Doug and me the most was on the distinctive features of unhealthy religious organizations. The authors listed ten characteristics of a toxic-faith system:

1. Members see themselves as unique and believe that their understanding of God makes them "special" in some way.

2. The leader is domineering and authoritarian.

3. A pervasive group mentality of "us versus them."

4. Toxic-faith systems are punitively controlling.

5. Members are expected to give tremendous service.

6. Many members in the system are physically ill, emotionally distraught, and spiritually dead.

7. Communication is from the top down or from the inside out.

8. Rules are distortions of God's intent and leave Him out of the relationship.

9. Religious addicts lack objective accountability.

10. The technique of labeling is used to discount a person who opposes the beliefs of the toxic-faith system.[2]

Doug and I debated as to whether or not Trinity fit all ten criteria, or just nine of the ten, but the description of the criteria was enough to jolt us again into discussing our continued involvement with the group. Regardless, any honest, objective look at the structure of Trinity Foundation, especially the excessive authoritarianism, was unsettling.

However, we believed that with our new understanding of toxic faith systems and spiritual abuse, we were equipped to redefine our relationship with the Trinity Foundation. We hoped that we could have an impact, as Mark had suggested, in changing the culture of the group. As it turned out, it was a foolish hope.

CHAPTER 11

✝

The Blow-up

"Trinity is hard on marriages," a former member said to me one evening over dinner. Doug and I had only been gone from Trinity Foundation about a month and it seemed that I was constantly confronted with new information that conflicted with my previously held beliefs about the group. After hearing that we had left the Trinity Foundation, Cary and his wife, Suzanne, had graciously invited Doug and me out to eat in a show of support over our decision.

"What do you mean?" I demanded. "There has only been one divorce at Trinity in the last twenty years. Ole says the divorce rate in Dallas is fifty percent or so. It is hard for marriages to survive *outside* of Trinity Foundation," I said, parroting the Trinity line.

"All I know is that my marriage to Suzanne has been much healthier since we left. During the time we were involved with the Trinity Foundation, we were constantly being split on issues whenever we would go to one of the elders for counseling. We are learning how to communicate with each other and discovering intimacy as a couple—something that we didn't have much time to do when we were at the Trinity—what with all the Bible studies and other activities. You'll understand what I'm talking about after you and Doug have been gone a while."

Former member Danielle revealed the fears that haunted her after she and her husband had left the group, "We thought our marriage could not survive if we were not a part of the Trinity Foundation. We had been told so many times that we couldn't succeed—that our marriage would crumble. I was scared to death when we left. Every year on our wedding anniversary, I would think, 'Okay, we've made it another year. Maybe our marriage can survive outside of Trinity. We left over twelve years ago and have been married sixteen years now, but I still continue to mark the years and reassure myself that we can make it outside of the Trinity Foundation. I actually think that we have a better marriage now because we have to work through things by ourselves without depending on others. Marriage is a union between two people and God. At Trinity, however, it was two people and the entire group. It made it much harder."

Betty, another former member, shared Danielle's sentiments: "When my husband and I were members of the Trinity Foundation, it felt like I was married to sixty-four people. If my husband and I had a problem, we had to talk about it in our Bible study group, and then we were bombarded by everyone's opinions and thoughts. If we had stayed at the Trinity Foundation, our marriage would not have lasted."

There's usually a "straw that breaks the camel's back," and looking back on it still causes me a sense of shame. Several months after we married, Doug's oldest daughter, Marsha, called from Florida. She was having marital problems and wanted to move to Dallas with her six-month-old baby, but she had no money, no transportation, and no job. One of Trinity's missions, which they prided themselves on, was assisting people who were homeless (or marginally so). Marsha fit that profile, and Doug talked with Ole about the possibility of Trinity helping his daughter until she could get on her feet. Doug had worked for the Trinity Foundation for eleven years, and I had worked for several years in a volunteer position as the business manager for *The Door*, Trinity's bimonthly publication. It did not seem unreasonable to ask Ole if Marsha and the baby could stay in one of the two vacant apartments that Trinity owned until she could find employment and save enough money for a place of her own; however, Ole did not agree. He told Doug that he wanted to keep the condominium available for out-of-town guests. The one-bedroom condominium, which was owned by the Trinity Foundation, was nestled among several other units owned or rented by other members of the group. It was directly across the street from the Trinity Foundation's office and on the same block where most of the community lived. Ole liked to have reporters and other visitors stay at the condominium so that they could experience the fullness of community life. It generally was only occupied for a few days each month.

The other available dwelling that was not occupied was what we called the "back house," a small studio-type of apartment behind the building which housed the community's dining facility, school, and rooms for the Levites. Doug thought Ole did not want Marsha to stay at that place because he was holding it open for one of the members who was an attorney. Ole had tried for years and years to convince Sam to move his law office to the block. Sam, who was already providing numerous pro bono hours for Trinity and its members, had always tactfully declined. Sam did not intend to move his practice, but that did not deter Ole from not wanting Doug's daughter to stay there temporarily. Ole's solution was for Marsha and the baby to move in with us. Doug tried to change Ole's mind, "But, Ole, Wendy uses our spare bedroom as her office for the work she does for *The Door*. We really don't have the room, and besides that, Wendy has a great deal of fear about my daughter coming to live with us because of her experience when her ex-husband's nephew came to live with them right after they married. My daughter has so many problems right now and I am concerned that it will put too much stress on our new marriage."

When Marsha first called to ask if we would help her move to Dallas, Doug and I discussed the possibility of her staying with us for a short time. I talked with Doug about my previous marriage and the strain that my ex-husband's young nephew placed on our marriage. The boy's mother had been diagnosed with bipolar disorder (commonly referred to as manic depression) and would often stop taking her medication, causing her to become mentally unstable. It was during one of these psychotic episodes that she abandoned Daniel (who was only eleven years old) the day before my ex-husband and I married. Neither my ex-husband nor I had any children, and I was, after all a mental health professional, so I thought, "No problem. We will be an instant family and live happily ever after." Little did I realize that being raised by a mother who was mentally ill had left Daniel with tremendous emotional problems, and being abandoned on several occasions throughout his short life had resulted in not only deep emotional scars, but also anger toward women. Daniel saw me as a threat to his relationship with his uncle and an outsider who had no business coming into his life. My experience in the mental health field proved to be useless in this personal arena. I couldn't be objective in the midst of the constant emotional upheavals, and my ex-husband and I separated after three years of marriage.

When the prospect of Marsha living with us was raised, old fears and memories of my past marriage surfaced. I talked with Doug about my concerns that I would not be able to deal with it. I felt like a hard-hearted, selfish, mean-spirited, uncompassionate person — but I was too scared that it might destroy our marriage. I experienced considerable guilt and self-incrimination, but the fear was even greater. Doug discussed the matter again with Ole, but he refused to consent to Marsha living in one of Trinity's available residences.

Interestingly, Ole and I had a disagreement when Marsha was thirteen years old. In a typical adolescence stage, Marsha had conflicts with her mother and stepfather and wanted to move to Dallas to live with her father. Doug was living with another Levite and Ole in a three-bedroom duplex located on the block, which would not have been able to accommodate a teenaged girl. At that time, Ole agreed that Marsha could move to Dallas, but stated that she would have to live with one of the Trinity Foundation families. The same two apartments, the condominium Ole liked for guests to stay in and the back house, were both available back then. I felt so strongly that Marsha should live with her father that I met with Ole to try to convince him to allow Doug to stay in one of those apartments with Marsha. I distinctly remember Ole telling me that I did not understand the concept of community and family. I had not yet moved to the block and did not realize that in Trinity Foundation's conceptualization all of the adults served as parental figures and, therefore, Marsha living with one of the families was consistent with that perspective. I felt, however, that because Marsha was going through a difficult adolescent period, it was important that she live with her father, but Ole was adamant that Marsha should live with the Jacksons. Now, six years later, Ole was equally as adamant that Marsha should live with her father.

I wondered if Ole was still upset with me over the confrontation I had with him six months earlier when Doug and I wanted to get married and this was his way of reminding me who was actually in control. But with no other apparent options, I had no choice but to agree that Marsha and the baby could come to live with us. Less than a month later, the situation blew up.

Marsha was able to obtain a job soon after she arrived in Dallas; however, with an infant son who was not yet sleeping through the night, it was difficult for her to get up the next morning and go to work. Having a vested interest in her not losing this job, I suggested that we all take turns getting up with Jason during the night to feed him or rock him back to sleep. Soon we were all tired and irritable. One Friday evening I came home from work totally exhausted. I looked around at the disarray in my house and it was more than I could handle. I asked Doug if we could go out to eat and to a movie. I also wanted him to talk to Marsha about washing the dirty bottles and clothes, along with cleaning her bedroom and bathroom. Marsha wanted to invite her sisters over and I wanted her to clean up her mess around the house.

Doug's children were a "hot button" with him. Within a year after his divorce, his ex-wife, Moira, had moved to Florida with their three young daughters. Shortly thereafter, Doug began working for the Trinity Foundation as a Levite. A Levite had no rights to himself and therefore, Doug had to go to Ole anytime there was a decision to be made about his children. As they were growing up, the girls would come to Dallas each summer, but on each occasion Doug would have to negotiate with Ole concerning when he could pick them up, where they could stay, and how long they could stay—not to mention a host of other issues. During the time that Doug was a Levite, he often felt powerless in his role as a father. If his children had any financial needs, Doug was required to go before the group and plead for money. He was always acutely aware that it was Ole and the group who decided whether or not his daughters should be helped, and it was the group that ultimately decided how much financial assistance would be provided.

When I did not want the girls to come over that evening, it touched Doug on a deep emotional level. Having been in an environment since his divorce, where he felt he had had no control, he became furious with me. A big argument ensued and Doug slammed the phone into the wall. That was my "hot button"—my ex-husband had been a violent and rageful person. Although what Doug did was just a display of frustration, I totally lost it and told Doug to leave the house so that I could be alone. At that point I just wanted some space.

Within the culture of the Trinity Foundation, any problem that an individual or a couple had was considered to be the entire community's problem. In true Trinity fashion, Doug went over to our Bible study leaders' house and told them about our fight. Garth and Jan immediately came over and walked into my house without knocking. In the Trinity community, the usual custom of knocking on someone's door and waiting to be invited into the home had been abandoned. The group walked in and out of each other's homes with no thought about privacy boundaries.

When Garth and Jan walked into my house to ask me what was going on, I told them that I did not feel like talking about it. I knew that was "murdering" them because in the Trinity system, to withdraw was the same as murder; however, with all the stress that I had been feeling since Marsha and the baby moved in (as well as the still strained emotions from Trinity's attitude toward our marriage), I did not want to discuss our problems with the Browns, so they left. I certainly did not want Jan reminding me that God would "kick my butt" if I married Doug.

I did want to talk to someone—a friend or one of my sisters—but when I went to pick up the telephone, Marsha was outside on the balcony talking on it. I waited a few minutes and then walked out on the balcony to see if she was still on the phone. In an admittedly ugly tone I asked,

"Are you going to stay on that phone all night?" Just as I said that, Marsha saw her father walking down the sidewalk back toward our house. She got off the phone, ran downstairs and out the door, by this time hysterically crying, "Why is Wendy being so mean to me?" Doug's response tore my heart. "She's crazy," he replied, not realizing that I was on the balcony and could overhear him. I knew that he did not mean it in the literal sense, but what was so painful was that it felt like he had formed an alliance with his daughter against me. I felt betrayed, hurt, and I overreacted.

"How can you say that, Doug?" I screamed from the balcony. "If I'm so crazy, you and Marsha can just leave. I don't want you here! Just get out!" Doug and Marsha left and walked back down to Garth and Jan's house. Later, someone from the community came and got some of their clothes. I waited for Doug to call me so that we could talk things through, but he did not call. Never in our seven-year relationship had we failed to work through an issue. We had had an agreement that we would never let a day pass without resolving any arguments. Doug was much better with relationships than I was, and he taught me a great deal about the importance of commitment and talking through disagreements till there was true understanding and forgiveness. Ninety-nine percent of the time, throughout our relationship, whenever we had a conflict, it was Doug who initiated the reconciliation, it was Doug who hammered things out and insisted that I talk things through with him. For the first time in our relationship, he did not call.

When I did not hear from him by the next morning, I believed that our marriage was over and in an act of desperation and stupidity, I called a locksmith to change the locks. When the locksmith showed up, it took all of five minutes for everyone in the community to know.

At some point that day (or maybe it was the next, I don't remember now), Doug and I did finally talk. Both of us were so angry that neither one of us could not see the other's perspective. "Why didn't you call me, Doug?" I asked. "Jan thought it would be better just to 'let you stew in your juices.'" It was at this moment that I knew our marriage had no possibility of survival if we stayed at Trinity. Whether they were conscious of it or not, I was convinced that Ole and the elders would sabotage our marriage. The teaching was always to go to someone who was offended or hurting, regardless of whose fault it was. The teaching was always to initiate reconciliation with one's brother or sister. Jan's statement was the antithesis of the doctrine. I felt a sadness I cannot describe.

Somehow, we managed to talk things through, and Doug moved back. Marsha and the baby moved in with a lady in the community who worked as a Levite. She had a two-bedroom apartment at the end of the block, which was paid for by Trinity. The lady's daughter was away at college and her husband was in a federal prison in Oklahoma for a white-collar crime. Ole decided that Marsha could live with Karen until she was able to save enough money to get her own apartment. Nevertheless, that was the end of my commitment to the Trinity Foundation. That was the end of my involvement with the group. It was over.

The inability to work through our pain—Doug's having to do with my kicking him out of the house, and mine having to do with my sense of betrayal—prompted us to seek professional help. Doug made an appointment with the therapist that he had seen on that one occasion before we married, and within a week, we were sitting in her office for marriage counseling. Although we had come specifically to work through this issue in our marriage, all roads kept leading back to Trinity. In a very indirect way, our counselor kept asking questions that made us examine our life in the community. Doug, at this point, was still committed to the Trinity Foundation; however, by the end of the second counseling session with Debbie, Doug began his journey out of the Trinity Foundation.

CHAPTER 12

✝

Shattered Believers

Learning to trust God again is a tremendous risk for individuals who leave spiritually abusive groups. Many former members question why a loving God could have allowed them to have become involved in a cultic community—consequently, letting them devote years of their life to a cause that they now see as worthless. They feel robbed of those lost years and missed opportunities. They feel abandoned by a god whom they think permitted their spiritual rape, while they were only seeking to understand his mysteries—the god they experienced in the cultic group they now want nothing to do with. Everything they once believed now seemed meaningless.

During the last six months that my husband and I were involved with Trinity Foundation, I began to feel that I had fallen into a spiritual abyss and that I had lost my connection to God. I no longer sensed an intimacy with Him. He seemed so far away and unreachable. "How could that be possible?" I asked myself. "I live in a faith community. I go to Bible studies three times a week. How could I have lost my relationship with God?" Although I did not know it at the time, Amanda also felt disconnected from God.

"I couldn't pray," she said. "One day I woke up and realized that it had been a long time since I had prayed. Not only had I not prayed, but I couldn't. My relationship with God had completely deteriorated. So when I went to Bible study that night—you remember how Bible study would always start out with the leader asking if anyone had anything to talk about—well, I shared with my group that I wasn't praying anymore and I was told that not praying was a good thing. Prayer was simply an attempt to manipulate God in an effort to get something from Him. Prayer was just talking to God about your problems or concerns, or whatever, and thus taking thought for self. Since a believer was not to take thought for self, my inability to pray indicated that I was not thinking of my own stupid needs or concerns, but it didn't feel good that I wasn't praying anymore. I felt that spiritually I was in a dry place—a place far away from the presence of God," Amanda explained.

I knew exactly what she was talking about. I too, at some point, had lost my capacity for prayer. After leaving the Trinity Foundation, it was years before I could pray again. Prayer, in Ole's theology, was about the individual trying to get something from God—using God as a cosmic Santa Claus. Besides that, praying to God was presumptuous. Ole's rationale was this: "Why would the God of the universe give a flip about you?" We were, after all, just a blob of protoplasm.

All of the former members that I interviewed told me similar things about the effect that the Trinity Foundation had on their spirituality. One ex-member, Lydia, recalled, "It was ten years before I was able to read my Bible again." Jack told me he had not been able to go to a church for the better part of a decade after he left. Moira also remembered how her relationship with God had been impacted: "After I left the group, my faith was considerably shaken. I had two Bibles and some notes that I had taken over the years, and I stuck them in the attic. For about two years, I couldn't even think about it and the truth is, I don't even know what I believe today. I can't even tell you that there is a God."

Former member Dave's remarks were perhaps the most disconcerting: "Every day that Ole Anthony goes on living is another day I know there is no God."

Mark summed up most of the former members' emotional and spiritual state: "Leaving the Trinity Foundation was ten times worse than a failed marriage because in a divorce you may lose a house and you may lose your money, but you don't lose your entire social structure or sense of purpose. When I left the group, for a while I seemed to have lost my sense of who I was and my relationship with God. It was an emotional H-bomb for me, and I had to begin rebuilding my life."

What kind of a spiritual leader damages individuals to such a degree that, after they leave, they have no desire to enter another church for years? What kind of church weakens an individual's belief system to the point that he is unable to pray? What kind of religious group so unravels a person's faith that he can no longer profess a belief in God?

No one wakes up one morning and decides to join a group that will be detrimental to his faith. No one wakes up and makes a conscious decision to give up his freedom of choice. When the realization that one is, in fact, a member of a thought-controlling, spiritually abusive cult, the confusion and shame are overwhelming. Not only is there an intense feeling of shame and confusion, but there is also an enormous impact on one's understanding of and relationship with God.

The following e-mail written to my outside friends and family two months after I left the Trinity Foundation only slightly revealed the psychological and emotional turmoil that I was experiencing:

Dear Family and Friends:

Well, thought I would update you on the status of Doug's and my transition out of the "cult." We continue to need your prayers and support. The last two months have probably been the most stressful of my life.

Doug and I have been reading all these books about spiritual abuse, cults, and mind and behavior control. We have been totally blown away with the similarities that we are discovering between other spiritually abusive groups/cults and the Trinity Foundation. We are also going to a counselor who is helping us process our feelings.

Our eyes have been opened to the manipulation that we have experienced and there is such a feeling of shame. Our big question is, "How in the world did we become involved in the Trinity Foundation?"

For Doug, it is much easier to understand. He was in college—and at that point in his life when he was trying to discover the "meaning of life." He met Ole who purported to have the answer, and Doug slowly got hooked. I was at a vulnerable point in my life: going through a divorce (for the second time), feeling like a failure, and still grieving over several spiritual disappointments. The group offered a body of believers, a community and a family who would love and care for you. It was very appealing.

I can see *now* how my belief system was being dismantled. Publicly discrediting and ridiculing susceptible individuals were powerful techniques that Ole used. One belief that I continue to struggle to hold on to is that God loves me. At Trinity Foundation, God was portrayed as a harsh deity who didn't care about individuals, who, in fact, hated them. Ole taught that God hated us and that it was arrogant for us to think that God would want to have a personal relationship with any individual believer. The only thing God cared about was the church and, of course, the only true church was Trinity.

We put our house up for sale and are in the process of looking for another place to live. Although we love our old house with the wonderful balcony where you can see part of the Dallas skyline, I finally agreed with Doug that there was no way that we could stay on the same block where most of the Trinity members lived.

For the most part, it is as if we do not exist to Trinity. Ole taught this crazy thing about "touching the dead body," and I guess no one wants to have anything to do with us since we are now "dead."

Well, I had better close. Thanks for being there.

Wendy

The transition out of the Trinity Foundation was one of the worst periods of my life. When I came to believe that the Trinity Foundation was a spiritually abusive religious cult, all of those feelings of being special—because I had been involved in a great and meaningful expression of Christianity—were gone. My whole sense of self had been wrapped up in the mission of the Trinity Foundation. The community had become my whole universe—my whole life—so much so that I felt that I had lost everything—my belief system, my family, my faith, and even my very sense of who I was. Before, I had been a part of a unique community. Now, I felt that I had no direction, no purpose, and no sense of who I was or what I believed.

For years after I left, my one remaining hope that my time in the group had not been totally in vain was the belief that at least the Trinity Foundation had done some good through its investigations and exposure of the televangelists. Ole had been outspoken in his criticisms of these ministers and Trinity Foundation had eventually taken on the role of watchdog of the televangelists. Ole surfaced as an "expert" in this arena in the early 1990s when Trinity Foundation provided investigative documents and videos for ABC's *PrimeTime Live* in an exposé of Reverend Robert Tilton and two other ministers, W. V. Grant and Larry Lea. All three ministers were pastors of churches in the Dallas area and were portrayed as charlatans who used religion to solicit donations from their television audiences. The implications against Reverend Tilton were undoubtedly the worst. Tilton was accused of being a total fraud who solicited prayer requests only as a guise to con donations out of his television audience. Trinity Foundation reportedly discovered thousands of unanswered letters written to Reverend Tilton requesting prayer, which had been discarded in a dumpster behind Tilton's bank in Tulsa, Oklahoma. Trinity Foundation alleged that the donations that had been included in the letters were taken out and the prayer requests were thrown away.

After the ABC program aired, Tilton denied the allegations and presented the protocol that his ministry used to process the prayer requests and donations. He explained that an elaborate system had been developed to ensure that each letter was carefully handled. The mail was delivered to a bank where it was opened under supervision. Financial gifts were recorded and the prayer requests were then sent to Tilton's headquarters in Dallas where they were hand delivered to Tilton's home for him to pray over. However, the *Prime Time Live* program and the numerous follow-up pieces that it spawned were so incriminating that it ultimately led to the decimation of Tilton's church and television ministry.

After Ole appeared on *Prime Time Live* with Dianne Sawyer in the first major network program on televangelists, Robert Tilton's ministry organization produced a videotape, *Prime Time Lies—Anatomy of an Exposé*, to refute the damaging allegations that had been made in the ABC broadcast. Tilton's videotape raised a number of disturbing questions about Ole and the integrity of his investigations of the televangelists. In the original *Prime Time Live* broadcast, the footage of the

trash dumpster that allegedly had held the discarded prayer
requests was behind a bank that was not the location of the
bank where Tilton's mail was sent. There was speculation that
these prayer requests that Ole and his crew had unearthed
had either been manufactured or had been obtained from
someone on the inside of Tilton's ministry. Other details
in Tilton's rebuttal further contradicted Ole's claims. J. C.
Joyce, attorney-at-law, who represented Robert Tilton in the
lawsuit against ABC and Ole Anthony stated:

> None of the prayer requests which Ole had in his
> possession could have ever been found at the time and
> place that he had sworn under oath that they had been
> found. In several instances, particular prayer requests
> were alleged to have been found before it had ever been
> mailed. The actual coded envelope the prayer request was
> contained in was produced and entered into evidence,
> the postmark proved the lie.

I personally did not see this program until after leaving the
Trinity Foundation, while gathering material for this book.
The first time that I viewed the tape, I cried and was unable
to continue watching it. It seemed to be a direct assault on
my last hope that there was some redeeming value in the
Trinity Foundation. The possibility that Ole's investigation
was fraught with deliberate misrepresentations of the facts
and that the prayer requests had been planted was troubling.
I had been proud to have belonged to a group that exposed
hypocrisy; however, I began to doubt the integrity of Ole and
his investigation. Although I attempted to uncover the truth,
I was never able to conclusively determine whether or not
Ole had staged the discovery of the prayer requests. Sufficient
doubt existed, though, to destroy what little hope remained
that there was anything commendable about the Trinity
Foundation. When I discussed with other former members

the possibility that Ole may have planted the prayer requests in the dumpster, where he later "discovered" them, they all replied in a similar fashion, "Well, Ole was certainly capable of doing that." None of the former members thought that such deception would be out of character.

In one discussion I had with Bob, a private investigator, who had been directly involved in investigating the authenticity of the *PrimeTime Live* program, I was confronted with yet another aspect that I had not considered. When I was describing the spiritual damage that had been done to former members of the Trinity Foundation, Bob replied, "Do you realize that because of Ole's investigation, other people, such as those in Tilton's church, were also hurt? Believers who were part of Tilton's ministry also had their faith shaken."

It had not occurred to me that I had been involved with something that had negatively affected other people's relationships with God. I had been an instrument through my tithes and donations to the Trinity Foundation and through my participation and tacit agreement of what Trinity Foundation was doing. I had been a part of damaging the faith of other believers.

Tilton's *Prime Time Lies* videotape was aired in multiple television markets throughout the United States for approximately six weeks before an attorney for Ole distributed a letter stating that the program those television stations were airing was libelous, effectively halting the further broadcasting of the show. Included with the attorney's letter was a press release from Trinity Foundation and the multi-page document, "Trinity Foundation's Responses to Accusations in Robert Tilton's 'PrimeTime Lies'" with some fifty or more "supporting" exhibits. The entire package sent out to the media was approximately one hundred seventy pages long. Included in Trinity's document was a brutal assault on one of its former members who had participated in Tilton's program. To refute this woman's allegations, Trinity Foundation attacked her credibility by including court papers concerning her divorce decree, an affidavit from a current member of the Trinity Foundation stating that she had confided in him that she had at one point been in a psychiatric hospital, and two other affidavits from group members that suggested that she had had an affair with another person in the group and left because of Trinity Foundation's "open refusal to endorse her illicit sexual activities."

While I could understand that the statements made by this former member would be upsetting to Ole and members of the Trinity Foundation, the denigration of this individual was ruthless and merciless. And, it contradicted what Ole taught. Ole often preached that the test of whether a person truly loved God was whether he would "lay down his life" for others. Laying down one's life for another meant that you put that person's interests above your own, that you gave up your right to protect yourself or your reputation. Clearly, Trinity Foundation's reaction to this former member and the Tilton program could hardly be called an act of love or an act of "dying to self" as Ole wrote in this excerpt:

> When you are forgotten, or neglected, or purposely provoked, and you don't sting and hurt with the insult or the oversight, but your heart is happy, being counted worthy to suffer for Christ—That is Dying to Self.

It was troubling that Trinity Foundation's response to Tilton's program was inconsistent with Ole's teachings. What Trinity Foundation did to the televangelists was exactly what Ole preached against. Ole often said that we should not judge other people because we do not know what God is doing. We might judge with our senses that some event or activity is wrong, but we cannot know how God is using that situation for His own purposes. Should not that same teaching apply to the televangelists? How can we judge whether or not God is using their ministry for His good?

One former member of the Trinity Foundation, Allan, had disagreed with Trinity Foundation's investigation of the televangelists while he was a member, and often tried to voice his misgivings about this activity. He had a good friend who had come to know God through Tilton's ministry, and he witnessed her confusion and doubts about God after the *PrimeTime Live* show aired. Allan's stance was that there was no teaching in the Bible that promoted the attack on other people in the body of Christ. In fact, when one of Jesus' disciples came to him with a complaint about a man who was "casting out demons," Jesus told him that if the man was performing miracles in the name of God, he should not be opposed. "Do not forbid him, for he that is not against you is for you" (Luke 9:50b, RSV). While researching this book, I spoke with several believers who felt that Trinity Foundation's "ministry" as the televangelist watchdog had done more harm than good to the body of Christ.

The reader may well ask, "Are you not doing the same thing by writing about the Trinity Foundation?" This was an issue I had to examine thoroughly while I was writing this book. My response would be that it is crucial to speak out against spiritual abuse. We are careful to teach and learn about sexual harassment and abuse so that lives are not ruined. Is it not also important to warn others of the dangers of religious abuse? We teach our children not to let anyone touch their bodies inappropriately, and we should also teach that no one has the right to touch our souls in a harmful way.

After being confronted with this new information on the televangelist investigations, I recalled a conversation that Doug had with an ex-member, who, in response to Doug's assertion that the Trinity Foundation's exposure of the televangelists had been beneficial, stated, "I disagree. There is nothing good in Ole; therefore, how can anything he does be good?"

The question of whether or not Ole was evil was one that came up often in conversations, as former members struggled to understand the Trinity experience. Danielle had these comments:

Of course, we have all witnessed that Ole has done evil things, but is he evil? These evil acts have caused other people to suffer by his lies, degradation, manipulation, cynicism, exploitation and otherwise damaging people's psyche and I believe that he did choose these techniques while saying it is all of God. Ole may have been damaged psychologically as a child or young adult, which influenced him to become a cult leader, but that does not excuse the abuse and suffering he has caused.

Can you say that he was just psychologically sick or damaged? Or simply that he just made mistakes? All of us, as human beings, are vulnerable to sin and temptation, but when we continually choose wrong over right, we become more vulnerable to the evil forces in the world and move away from God. Ole's mind, which can only be analyzed by his actions, portrays that there are evil forces in his life that affect his decision-making abilities.

So, to answer the question is Ole evil? No, but he is influenced by evil forces that are powerful. I believe that a person can choose wrong over right to the point where he becomes so infested with evil that he is unredeemable. Of course, I cannot judge whether Ole or anyone else has gotten to that point. The only thing we can do is to pray for him that he does not continue to abuse others in the name of God.

Another issue that was debated among the former members was whether Trinity Foundation was flawed from the beginning or whether it had simply gotten off track at some point. Some members believed that Trinity Foundation was pure and good at its initial inception, but had eventually become a different place from the one to which they originally were attracted. Some felt it was the era of the hot seats, where members' spirits were crushed, leaving them in a dependent, vulnerable state, that transformed the organization. Others felt that it was advent of the televangelist investigations that changed the leader and, ultimately, the spirit of the group.

On the other side of the debate were those who strongly believed that Trinity Foundation was doomed from the onset because of the personality of the leader, his lack of a formal theological training, and the absence of a viable structure of accountability. On the last point, Ole, of course, would say that he was accountable to his elders and the board of directors; however, I witnessed too many times when the board or the elders rubberstamped whatever action Ole was advocating that the foundation take. I observed firsthand the incredible pressure that was exerted on anyone who was brave enough to oppose one of Ole's ideas.

The possibility that Trinity Foundation was flawed from the beginning was a concept that troubled many former members. As Dave stated, "If Trinity Foundation was flawed from the beginning, what does that say about me? I was flawed?" His response illustrated the necessity that former members must work through the shame of being involved with a cultic group and realize that it was their idealism that made them susceptible to the siren call of the leader. Mark recalled that after he left the group, another former member gave him the book, *Combatting Cult Mind Control*, by Stephen Hassan. "I had moved into an apartment by myself and I remember I started reading this particular book and highlighting everything in yellow that I could relate to. I was horrified when I realized that most of the book was yellow. That was when I began to realize just what I had been through. Like most people, I was not willing to admit (at first) that I had been a part of a cultic group, but the evidence was overwhelming."

The questions of how we became involved in an authoritarian cultic group, how we allowed someone else to control our lives, how we came to believe that the leader had the right to control, and other such questions, were the most troubling issues that we former members faced upon leaving the Trinity Foundation. We spent considerable time analyzing and contemplating all of these questions. We examined every aspect, looked at it from every conceivable angle, and in the end, realized that the questions were unanswerable. In our healing, the questions had to change. The questions no longer were concerned with understanding our own vulnerabilities that led to involvement in a religiously abusive cult or the attempts to understand the cult leader in terms of whether he was evil or not. At some point, the questions became: How do we get through the pain and confusion of the experience? How can this experience be used? Would we allow God to use this chapter of our lives in our spiritual journey, or would we forever be stuck in our shame and humiliation? The Trinity experience was a traumatic event in our lives and would forever change us and affect the way we saw the world.

CHAPTER 13

Aftermath

The psychological effects of leaving the Trinity Foundation persisted long after I had physically severed my ties with the group. Not only was there a feeling of emptiness, but also the fear of losing God and not being able to survive outside of the Trinity Foundation haunted most of my waking hours. Because a fear had been instilled in me that I would not be able to "make it" outside of the group, I often felt traumatized.

Moreover, I realized that I had adopted Trinity Foundation's worldview, and I would have to rethink my entire belief system. This would prove to be quite difficult because the experience at Trinity Foundation had had an effect on my cognitive abilities and I no longer trusted my own judgment and decision-making skills. I no longer had any basis for thinking, judging, or choosing. I felt I had no way to think about myself or how I should act — nor any means even to consider religion or who God was. I had been taught to doubt everything that I was, and I had come to believe that I could not trust my own mind or my judgment. I did not even have the slightest idea about how to frame a question to myself or to anyone else. All I was left with was an overwhelming state of confusion.

I heard Ole's voice in my mind a thousand times a day. I felt so infected by him that even my own thoughts seemed like poison to me. I felt like nothing, with no life of my own. The years spent at Trinity had cost me my individuality, my awareness of self, and my unique sense of personal identity.

Additionally, the feeling of estrangement from people I had grown to know and love, and the disillusionment about what I had hoped was a genuine community of believers, left me flailing. But the real hurt came when I began to doubt every relationship that I had ever had. After leaving Trinity Foundation, I realized that my trust in myself, my trust in others, as well as my trust in God had been broken. I went through a period of being scared of people. When Doug and I would visit churches, people would come up and talk with us, and I did not know how to interact with them. Even when old friends would call, I often found myself not wanting to talk to them. People who had not shared the experience had difficulty relating to the intensity of the loss and its long-lasting effects, and I did not have the words to explain what I was feeling. I no longer had a language to express myself, because the Trinity language did not fit. I was preoccupied with Trinity, and yet I could not talk about my experience with friends or family. At the same time, I desperately needed to talk.

Part of what was so difficult about talking to people is that they would say things like, "Christians wouldn't get involved in cults if they would only realize how important it is to know scripture." Well, I knew scripture. Prior to joining the Trinity Foundation, I had spent years studying the Bible. I had earned a master's degree from Southwestern Baptist Theological Seminary, a conservative institution. Doug was also familiar with the Bible prior to joining Trinity

Foundation. Our falling into a cult was not the result of a lack of scriptural knowledge.

I do not know how I would have gotten through that period if I had truly been alone—if I had not been married to Doug. Many nights we spent hours talking and sorting through our thoughts and feelings. Since he had shared the experience with me, we could use Trinity jargon and not have to explain what we meant. I also did not have to worry that he would judge me for having become involved there in the first place.

Shortly after we left the foundation, we put our house up for sale and, in what I saw as an affirmation from God that we were doing the right thing, we had a contract on the house within thirty days after putting it on the market. My father-in-law, Gordon, who is a real estate agent, went with me as I looked at house after house. Early in the process, Doug had tired of house-hunting and had asked me to tell him when I had narrowed the search down to two or three houses. Gordon patiently lined up houses for me to look at and, looking back on it, part of the reason it took me so long to decide on one house was my lack of confidence in my deci-sion-making abilities. In a lot of ways, it was also therapeutic, because it allowed me time to think about something other than Trinity. After several months, we decided on a home and moved out, east of Dallas, to a small suburb that was closer to my work.

When we moved away from the block, I experienced a loneliness that is hard to describe. Doug had begun working on a graduate degree in counseling and was working full-time in retail, so often when I came home from work, he was either at his job or in class. As a result, there were many hours when I was alone and lonely. When I had lived on the block, there were always people around. All you had to do was go outside your home and there would be someone with whom you could talk. Or you could always go down to the Lair, eat dinner, and have as much social interaction as you wanted. And, there were Bible studies three nights a week. When we moved to Rowlett, however, it was not the same. I exchanged e-mails and talked for hours on the phone to Crystal, another former Trinity Foundation member who left around the same time that we did. Many nights I would come home and not know what to do with myself. I remember calling Crystal one night and asking her, "What do people do when they don't live in a community and don't go to Bible study all the time?"

And then there was the anger. I went through a period where I was so angry. Anger was an emotion at Trinity Foundation that indicated that one felt like a victim. "There are no victims in the Kingdom of God," Ole would proclaim. At Trinity Foundation, we were taught that we were not victims. Being a victim was considered the most self-absorbed, self-centered, antichrist attitude that a believer could exhibit. Several months after I moved to the block, I accepted a position as the director of a rehabilitative program for offenders with mental illness. The politics and the community dynamics inherent in this program were very difficult, and I often felt that I was in an impossible situation. Every time I tried to talk about it in my Bible study, I was told by my Bible study teachers that I was playing the victim. Basically, any time someone voiced a complaint or tried to talk about a problem he was experiencing, the group would admonish him for acting like a victim. Everything was just as God wanted it to be, so if an individual was having any difficulties, it was because he was refusing to see that the situation was ordained by God.

Dr. Paul R. Martin, a licensed psychologist and executive director of Wellspring Retreat and Residential Center (a treatment facility that specializes in helping individuals who have left cults), wrote:

In coming to grips with what has happened to the ex-cultist, it is quite helpful to employ the victim or trauma model. According to this model, victimization and the resulting distress it causes are due to the shattering of three basic assumptions that the victim held about the world and the self. These assumptions are the belief in personal invulnerability, the perception of the world as meaningful, and the perception of oneself as positive. The former cult member has been traumatized, deceived, conned, used, and often emotionally and mentally abused while serving the group or the leader. Like other victims of such things as criminal acts, war atrocities, rape, and serious illness, ex-cultists often reexperience the painful memories of their group involvement. Trauma also causes many to lose interest in the outside world, feel detached from society, and display limited emotions. [1]

When I read this passage four months after I left Trinity Foundation, I cried and was amazed at how sensitive I continued to be. Dr. Martin's explanation made sense, but the victim label had such a negative connotation for me. It had been drilled in my head that to think of myself as a victim was evil. You were not to express any hurt that was felt over someone else's behavior towards you or risk being reprimanded. To think that I was a victim of a cult or religiously abusive group was antithetical to everything that I had come to believe during my years at Trinity Foundation.

The truth is that the expression of anger was a part of my recovery — the process of taking back control of my life. It was a healthy expression of self-caring. It was hard to see God as willing to love me and protect me from harm if I was not willing to be angry that I had been hurt. Until I could come to terms with the fact that I was in fact a victim, it was difficult to become a survivor.

Madeline Tobias, a psychotherapist who has worked with ex-cult members and who co-authored *Captive Hearts,*

Captive Minds, contributed a chapter in *Recovery from Cults* (Langone, editor, 1993). On the subject of anger, she wrote:

> Emerging anger is one of the first signs of recovery from the cult experience. Anger is a normal and healthy reaction to the numerous harms and assaults perpetrated upon us. Anger is the most appropriate response to the abuse and manipulations of the cult and is also the hardest for some ex-members to get in touch with and deal with. Anger means you are now ready to acknowledge that you were victimized. That is incredibly painful. What was done was heinous, evil. Ex-members are entitled to their rage. [2]

During the time that I was in this stage (although the grief process is not linear), I wrote a series of "Grinch" stories. Some of the titles were: "How The Grinch Stole Cindy Lou's Wedding," "How The Grinch Stole Christmas," "How The Grinch Stole the Sheep," and "How The Grinch Stole Easter." I even called them anger expressions number one, number two, etc. One of these stories is provided below:

How The Grinch
Stole Cindy Lou's Wedding

Cindy Lou had been dating Doug Who, one of the inhabitants of the Isle of Columbia, for several months when the topic of marriage came up. "If we ever get married, the Great Grinch and his followers will have to approve it, and there will be a great celebration," said Doug Who. "What do you mean, the Great Grinch will have to approve it?" Cindy Lou asked. "That's the way that it is done on the great Isle of Columbia, Cindy Lou. Just like in the olden days, the family of the groom and the family of the bride decide that their son and daughter are to be married and prepare for the celebration."

Cindy Lou thought this to be very strange, but she reasoned in her mind that since her two previous marriages had not worked out, maybe it was wise to wait on the counsel of others. In fact, her good friend, Victoria, told her that she was prepared not to marry her fiancé if her friends had not approved of him. "Friends know us best," Victoria said. So Cindy Lou decided that giving her judgment to a wiser body regarding whom and when she married would keep her from repeating her mistakes.

In the fall of 1993, Cindy Lou attended a wedding on the Isle of Columbia. It was the most beautiful and spiritual wedding celebration that she had ever attended. The whole isle celebrated and toasted the Bride. Cindy Lou understood more clearly the analogy of Christ and His Bride, the Church, through the wedding events that took place on the isle. She longed for the day when she and Doug Who could experience it. She thought of her family and friends and how wonderful it would be for them to be a part of this special ceremony.

After years of dating, Cindy Lou found herself more in love with Doug Who than ever before — and was confident that he was the one with whom she wanted to spend the rest of her life. By this time, Cindy Lou had moved to the Isle of Columbia and although not a perfect follower, a follower, nonetheless, of the Great Grinch.

One day Doug Who approached the Great Grinch and inquired whether or not he and Cindy Lou could receive the Blessing and be married. "Cindy Lou has only been here three years!! She doesn't even understand the great doctrine that we teach here on the isle!!! She will only bring you destruction, Doug Who!" exclaimed the Grinch. Another year passed and Doug Who went again to the Great Grinch to see if he would grant their marriage wish. "No, no. This is not the right time.

Cindy Lou is miserable in her job and would make a horrible wife!" the Great Grinch proclaimed.

Yet another year went by and Doug Who thought it was the perfect time to marry Cindy Lou. They had now been dating for five years. Cindy Lou had a new job—and was very happy there. Everything seemed to be going well. Doug Who made another visit to the Great Grinch to ask for the Marriage Blessing. The Great Grinch thundered, "Did you forget that your teenage daughter is coming to live with you? How can you take on that responsibility and a new wife? The timing is not right, Doug Who."

Doug Who's daughter left after a year, and Doug Who went again to the Great Grinch to seek the Marriage Blessing. "Why are you not content, Doug Who? We have taken you in and given you a place to live. We give you eighty dollars a week for the sixty-seventy hours of work you perform each week. You have a spiritual problem, Doug Who. If you cannot be content with where you are, how can you be content in a marriage? Besides, Cindy Lou just bought a house on the isle, and that's not the best time to get married."

Over and over, Doug Who would make a trip to the High Place of the Great Grinch to see if the Great Grinch would grant the Blessing. Each time he was told that it was not the right time, he was not right, or that Cindy Lou was not right. "It would be a disaster if I gave you the Marriage Blessing, Doug Who!" the Great Grinch declared on many occasions.

One day after Doug Who and Cindy Lou had been dating for almost seven years, Doug Who began to question whether the Great Grinch even had the Blessing to give. The Great Grinch seethed with anger and said, "I am sick unto death of you two! I don't give a Rat's Ass if you get married!!" But I will not give you My Great Blessing!! I will not marry you, and I will not allow the inhabitants of the Isle of Columbia to attend!"

Finally, Doug Who and Cindy Lou realized that they had been seeking the Blessing from the wrong source. All these years they had believed that the Great Grinch was the holder of the Blessing, but the Great Grinch only had a grinch blessing to give, and grinch blessings have no real worth. The true Blessing, the only Blessing that has worth, the only Blessing that was ever needed was from their Father.

On March 24, 2000, Doug Who and Cindy Lou received the Marriage Blessing.

Most people feel very uncomfortable when anger is expressed, and often when I went off on a tangent about the Trinity Foundation, I would be urged to forgive. Forgiveness is important — and is certainly a part of the recovery process; however, it cannot be short-circuited. At the same time, I was still struggling with Ole's definition of forgiveness. His definition was, "Forgiveness means you defend the other person's right to have done what he or she did." Ole did not believe there was a permissive will of God. Everything that happened to you was by direct design of God, so any action or behavior toward you was exactly what God planned, and therefore, was perfect.

Dr. Martin discussed the healing aspect that anger can produce in the following extract from, "Post-Cult Recovery: Assessment and Rehabilitation:"

> It is vital that ex-members' moral outrage not be treated as pathological. They have been wronged. They have been made to feel helpless. Their former sense of right and wrong — one of the most central elements of the human identity — has been turned upside down. Rage fortifies the weakened remnant of their moral self against the lingering power of the cultic evil. The job at being free and the rage

that comes with understanding what happened serve to clean the human spirit. These feelings must run their course. At this point, recovery to post-cult life begins.[3]

I began the difficult journey of recovery from my cult experience—to recapture my sense of self and my understanding of God—and embarked on a quest to discover the answers to my questions. But that quest did not come without considerable difficulty and did not begin until almost three years after I had left. The quest was simply this: to believe in a God of love. All I really needed was to know with all my heart and within my spirit that I was loved by Him. The doctrine of "God hates you" that Ole taught had infiltrated my belief system, and although, intellectually I knew it was a false teaching, emotionally I somehow still believed that I was a nonentity to God.

An e-mail Crystal sent me shortly after Doug and I broke away from the group sums up the frustration she experienced from the constant emphasis that Trinity Foundation placed on our evil nature:

Wendy,

I'm so tired of hearing from anyone, in any form, "bad dog, bad dog." I have been struggling with the message that Trinity Foundation gave us concerning how evil we were and how God hated us. How long can a person hear that message without falling into the pit of despair? Why was all the focus on how incredibly sinful we were?

Probably the hardest thing for me is what Trinity made of prosperity gospel preachers and what evil things they were doing by teaching about God's blessings. What was wrong with focusing on the goodness of God instead of always emphasizing that God hated us? Why couldn't we talk about the joy and blessings of God? Couldn't we be trusted with them?

I found a passage in Numbers 6:22–27, which lately resonates in my being like a loud echo and runs to places in my heart undiscovered:

"… The Lord bless thee, and keep thee: The Lord make his face to shine upon thee, and be gracious unto thee: The Lord lift up his countenance upon thee, and give thee peace. And they shall put my name upon the children of Israel, and I will bless them."

Why couldn't we have ended Bible study, feasts, fasts, and each and every Big Group with that? Couldn't we be trusted with it? There was so much liturgical trashing and crashing at Trinity that I struggled to see God as a loving, caring, Father who only wants the best for me.

Anyway, there's part of my struggle. It goes on but I truly believe this leg of the journey is about knowing God's blessings. That's part of the deal, right? From sin and death comes everlasting life — everlasting life like only God can provide. Can we be trusted with it? Yes.

Love,
Crystal

Crystal,

I cried when I read your e-mail. Ole didn't think we could be trusted with the joy and blessings of God. I remember saying on many occasions, at yet another Bible study on "the cross," "What about the joy? When do we get to talk about the joy of our salvation? The blessings that the Father has for us?" My Bible study teachers would rebuke me and say I was just about the "theology of glory."

There was so much emphasis on the sinfulness of man and God's hatred of us that I struggle with all of that today. Yes, God hates sin, but the Bible says that while we were yet sinners, Christ died for us. Our sermon at church last week was on Luke 15 where Jesus talked about the shepherd who lost one of his sheep. He left his other ninety-nine sheep to go find the lost one. That touched me. Doesn't that show that God loves the individual — you and me? And, as with Jabez, won't He bless us when we come to Him in the full assurance that He is our protector, our father, the only source of our joy?

I don't want Ole's god. I want to know God for who He really is. I need to figure out what I believe today at this point in my spiritual journey.

And yes, we can be trusted with it.

Wendy

Dear Wendy,

Ahhhh. But to imagine a loving God. I remember thinking during Bible study the same thing, "Enough of the cross! Where's the joy?"

But I never came out and asked about it. I kept thinking we would get there, but we never did.

Crystal

This "leg of the journey" as Crystal had written is, for me, about knowing the God of love. Crystal died at the age of forty-one about a year after she wrote that e-mail. I have no doubt that today she is truly experiencing the God of love — in His very presence — and that she is praying that while I am still here on this earthly trail, I will completely come to know this loving God.

I am almost done with one aspect of that original journey: regaining an understanding of who I am. Of course, now comes the difficult part of articulating it so that it might be of use to others. But at least I have a sense of who I am now, a sense of self. Which belongs to no one. Which is my own.

CHAPTER 14

✝

Hope for the Hopeless

There is a story about two people who rode the same bus from work. Each day the woman got off the bus at a cemetery. Day after day, a man who also rode this bus observed her getting off at the cemetery. He thought to himself, "What grief is this woman going through that she must stop every day and visit the gravesite?" One day he mustered the courage to ask her and she replied, "Oh, son, I'm not visiting the cemetery. I live on the other side of the cemetery and must go through the cemetery to get home."

In order to get "home," to come to a place of peace and healing, former members of spiritual abuse must go through the "cemetery." To fully heal, ex-cult members must go through the grief recovery process and work through the deep sense of loss—loss of a vision, loss of relationships, loss of faith, loss of commitment to an important spiritual cause, and loss of a way of life. After my involvement with the Trinity Foundation, I wanted nothing more than to forget my experience there and to pretend somehow that it had not happened—or at least that it did not have an impact on me. At the same time, I was unable to forget. I could not numb the pain, because the sense of loss and confusion would not go away. I tried to bury it deep inside, but it kept sneaking out. Nightmares. Depression. Anger. Confusion. Distrust of others. I needed to heal, but I did not know how to do it.

In their book, *Captive Hearts Captive Minds: Freedom and Recovery from Cults and Abusive Relationships,* authors Madeleine Tobias and Janja Lalich point out that each person's experience in a cultic group is different and, therefore, the aftereffects are dependent on a number of factors, such as the length of time the individual was involved with the group, and the degree of spiritual or psychological manipulation that was exerted on the individual. Additionally, personality factors like sensitivity, emotional resilience, and affiliation needs have an effect on the individual's recovery and healing. Tobias and Lalich recommend a psychoeducational approach to promote healing and a healthy transition out of a cult. [1] This is a process of gathering knowledge and understanding of the cult experience and is a critical part of working through the shame and humiliation of finding yourself in a spiritually abusive group.

What the recovery process looks like will vary from individual to individual; however, it is imperative that the ex-cult member develops an understanding of the dynamics of his group and realizes that the process takes time. After leaving the Trinity Foundation, Doug and I spent a great amount of time reading literature about cults. We not only read books by survivors of cults and spiritual abuse, but also books by cult experts. These books were extremely beneficial in our struggle to understand how and why we became involved and why we stayed for so many years.

The majority of the cult experts recommended professional help, so Doug and I returned to the therapist he had met with before we married. Finding a good therapist is not an easy task, but God in His grace led us to the perfect counselor. Although Debbie did not have any experience in working with cult victims, she did have expertise in working with women in abusive relationships, and thus was able to relate to the spiritual abuse we had experienced. Debbie was a gift from God and proved to be a major instrument in our recovery process. She told us at one point that her counseling sessions with us required more prayer prior to each session than anyone else she was seeing at that time. Because she was a Christian, she did not view our religious interest as something unhealthy. Additionally, she did not subscribe to the theory that we had become involved in a cult because we were psychologically defective prior to joining the Trinity Foundation. She recognized our unique vulnerabilities that made us susceptible to a community like Trinity Foundation, but she focused our counseling sessions on how the practices and the belief system we had adopted were affecting us now.

In addition to professional counseling, Doug and I also found the support of former members to be extremely helpful. While still at Trinity Foundation, we often heard about ex-members getting together and were critical of their affiliation with one another. After Doug and I left Trinity, we found ourselves doing exactly what we had criticized them for doing. We sought out former members. We needed them. We needed to know what their experience had been and how they transitioned out of the group. We needed to talk about our feelings, and who better to talk with than people who had experienced the same thing. About a year after we left Trinity, we started, along with another couple, something we called "Third Saturday." It was a monthly get-together of former members and provided an opportunity to reconnect with one another. These were people we had come to know and love, but when individuals or families left Trinity Foundation, inevitably the relationship was broken. Although Ole never explicitly told us not to associate with former members, we knew it was not acceptable—primarily because it might prevent them from returning. Individuals who left the group were in a state of rebellion and if you contacted them, you were somehow enabling or encouraging them.

We wanted to rebuild our friendships, which was why "Third Saturday" was begun. Of course, Trinity Foundation soon learned of this monthly gathering, which they discounted as "Trinity bashing sessions." That was not the intent of the group, but often, critical things were said about Trinity. It was a way of processing our experience and healing from the pain of it.

Most cultic groups develop words or phrases that are unique to them and carry specific meanings. Trinity Foundation was no exception. A group's special jargon provides its members with a feeling of exclusiveness and a sense of mystical enlightenment. Robert Lifton, a prominent psychiatrist and author, used the term *loaded language* in his book, *Thought Reform and the Psychology of Totalism*. He explained how the use of clichés and exclusive phrases impact an individual's critical-thinking abilities. [2] One of Ole's common phrases was, "If you could see in the Spirit," which implied that whomever he was talking with obviously could not see in the Spirit. This terminology was often used to discount or dismiss a question or thought of one of his followers, and was actually quite effective at shutting down a discussion. With this simple device, Ole could always trump the other person with a higher level of truth that only he could see. Another term that was frequently used at the Trinity Foundation was abiding. If you did not like a situation, you were to abide anyway. If you had a problem with another member, you were admonished to abide. Abiding was proof that you were at peace with God.

Loaded words generally have strong emotional overtones and can evoke intensely negative reactions—"scary" words to quote Kathleen Norris in her book, *Amazing Grace, a Vocabulary of Faith*. Norris describes how she left the faith of her childhood, and during her adult years, began a journey back to recapture her faith in God. In trying to make her way back to God, Kathleen talks about her efforts in redefining religious phrases and stated, "a struggle I only endured because I dared hope that eventually the words wouldn't seem like "theirs," but also "mine."[3] After we left Trinity Foundation, I realized that part of the Trinity legacy was "scary" words—words that triggered unpleasant memories or heretical beliefs. I am still working through them and echo Kathleen's statement of only enduring it because I dare hope that the words will become mine again.

In addition to reclaiming words and "unloading the language" as cult experts advise, reframing who God is may be the single most important step in the recovery process. Dr. Martin stated in his article, "Dispelling the Myths: The Psychological Consequences of Cultic Involvement," that spiritual problems are often present in ex-cult members; however, the spiritual problems "generally originate with the group's unbiblical teaching rather than having their source in the individual's own relationship with God." In his experience, almost all former members of religious cults or extremist sects are "confused about such things as the grace of God, the nature of God, submission to authority, and self-denial." Dr. Martin goes on to say that "it is noteworthy that groups with widely varying doctrinal stances … uniformly distort God's grace and character."[4] Thus, an essential step in the recovery process is rethinking the group's theological, intellectual, and ethical practices and beliefs.

Reestablishing my relationship with God was the most difficult task in my recovery process. It has been a monumental task in my spiritual pilgrimage—one in which I continue to struggle. After my husband and I left the Trinity Foundation, we were encouraged by a good friend and former member to "find a way to stay connected to God." Matthew explained that he left Trinity Foundation twice. The first time he separated from the group he eventually went back because he had not been able to fill the spiritual void that he felt after he left. When he broke away the second time, he and his wife found a loving Catholic church and received spiritual counseling from a wise priest, which was instrumental in their healing process.

After leaving the Trinity Foundation, I visited different churches each Sunday. Not knowing anything other than the Southern Baptist denomination and Bible churches, I gravitated toward evangelical churches. Each time I attended this type of worship service, I heard Ole's critical and mocking voice. When an individual or a group of vocalists stood on the platform at the front of the sanctuary and sang, I would hear Ole contemptuously talking about how the modern church is focused on entertainment. Or during the time when members greeted each other, I would hear Ole ridiculing this activity and telling us that churches today know nothing about true community. I wanted desperately to be able to go to a church and experience God, but Ole's words flooded my mind and poisoned any experience of worship. Week after week I would attend yet another church, but I was beginning to lose hope — that I wouldn't be able to find God again.

During the time I visited various churches, Doug told me that he could not go with me to an evangelical church. "Ole ruined them for me, Wendy," he explained. He suggested that we try a liturgical church, such as Catholic or Episcopal. Eager to find a church that we could attend together, I located an Episcopal church near our home. One Sunday morning we went to the early worship service at All Saints Episcopal Church. There were only a handful of people at this service, and we hoped that we would not stand out since we did not have a clue about the protocols in the worship service. When the time for communion came, the congregants gathered at the altar. Doug and I sat there watching.

In an apparent departure from the formality that had encompassed the service, the priest came out from behind the rail of the altar and asked if we wanted to take communion with them. Doug answered that we were not members of the Episcopal Church. Father Ray replied, "We invite all baptized believers to have communion with us." My husband had tears in his eyes as we went to the altar and kneeled to take the Holy Eucharist. Later, Doug told me that the priest's words had a powerful effect on him. "On some level, I thought that leaving Trinity Foundation was synonymous with leaving the faith. Although I intellectually knew that I was a believer, Ole's teachings over the years left me fearful that I was now one of those "almost disciples," forever separated from God. When Father Ray invited us to take communion, I felt that here was a place where I was welcomed as a fellow believer."

Unlike the churches I had previously attended, in the Episcopal church people generally do not talk to each other before the service, but rather use the time for personal reflection and preparation for worship. Upon entering the church, there is an air of reverence and it is customary for individuals to bow to the altar in recognition of Christ the King before sitting down on the pew. At the front of the church are the altar and the cross, which focus one's attention on the purpose of worship. Near the altar are candles symbolizing the Light of the world, Christ Jesus. The outer candles are lit at the beginning of the service as a reminder of the illumination of God's Word. The inner candles are not lit until the consecration of the bread and wine to symbolize the presence of Christ. Everything about the service prepares the individual to center on the worship of God.

A liturgical church proved to be what both Doug and I needed at this juncture of our journey back to God. I had lost the capacity to pray while I was at Trinity Foundation. I had a deep need to worship, but I no longer had the words or method by which to do so. However, in this Episcopal church the means to worship was given to me—in the scripture readings, the spoken prayers, and in the Holy Eucharist. The liturgy gave me a way to worship God once again.

Additionally, we needed a place where we felt safe—a place that would accept all our doubts, confusion, and questions, and patiently allow us to sort through our beliefs. We found that refuge at All Saints Episcopal Church. In some of the cult literature, the experts suggest that the ex-member find a church that is radically different from their cultic group. Our new pastor was the polar opposite of Ole. Father Ray Ball was a church historian with extensive education. He was a humble man with a servant's heart—and exactly the type of minister we needed during this period of our spiritual healing.

During the first year after I left Trinity Foundation, I found it hard to get through a worship service without crying at least once. A song, a scripture passage, or something in a sermon would trigger a memory of Trinity Foundation and tears would stream down my face. I was always embarrassed by how sensitive I was, but my need to attend a worship service was too strong to be concerned about what others thought if they saw me crying. I recall one time when the congregation sang "Amazing Grace," and I could not stop crying. It was one of Ole's favorite songs and I realized I could not sing it. Although it had been my grandfather's favorite song too, I never wanted to hear it again. I learned later in reading the cult literature that this phenomenon was known as "triggering" and refers to an overpowering emotion that arises when an internal or external stimulus sparks a memory, a teaching, or a state of feeling from one's cultic experience. Discovering that those triggers are normal and usually temporary helped me understand that I was not "losing it" or going crazy. Understanding them was important in the recovery process.

Rethinking practices, such as the celebration of holidays, is yet another task for the ex-cult member. At Trinity Foundation, Ole taught that Christmas was a pagan holiday only celebrated by the ignorant and weak of faith. "Jesus was not born on Christmas!" Ole would often say. "Jesus was conceived on Hanukkah and born on Rosh Hashanah." When I became involved with the group, there were no outward manifestations of the Christmas season. The customary practices of putting up decorations, hanging lights, or displaying Christmas trees were ridiculed, although a number of the members celebrated the secular custom of exchanging gifts — primarily, for the enjoyment of the children. During the time I was there, Ole had a new girlfriend, Suzette, who was instrumental in changing this Trinity convention and Christmas decorations started appearing during the holiday season. By this time, however, I had adopted Ole's belief that Christmas was not when Jesus was born and demonstrated my disdain by not celebrating Christmas except to exchange gifts with my family members.

Rather than celebrating Christmas as a religious observation, Trinity Foundation members observed Hanukkah and Rosh Hashanah. On Hanukkah, each of the Bible study groups gathered on a Sunday afternoon and read Old Testament scriptures and passages from the Book of Enoch, (an extra-canonical book), and Jubilees, and Judith (books in the Old Testament Apocrypha). Later during the day, all the groups came together for "Big Group" during which the children of Trinity Foundation would perform their annual play and act out the story of Judith.

The tale of Judith takes place during the reign of Nebuchadnezzar over Assyria. Judith saves her people from an assault by the Assyrian army by seducing the general, getting him drunk, and chopping off his head. Each year during Hanukkah, the children acted out the story and especially loved the part where a head was carried off on a platter. I always thought this was one of Trinity Foundation's oddest events and after leaving commenting on it to my friend, Amanda, whose response was, "Thanks, Wendy, for reminding me that I had my children in a cult."

The first Christmas after leaving Trinity Foundation occurred several months after Doug and I severed our ties with the group. It had been years since I celebrated Christmas as the birth of my Savior and had grown accustomed to seeing Christmas from Ole's perspective because of his authoritarian, emphatic insistence that Christmas was pagan worship. Prior to joining Trinity Foundation, I had always loved Christmas. To me, it was a special time of reflection and celebration of the Savior, my Savior. I cherished this time of universal observation of His birth when the whole world recognized that the King had been born, the One who would take away the sins of the world.

Our first Christmas away from the Trinity Foundation almost slipped by us, but fortunately, during one of our counseling sessions, our therapist asked my husband and me about our plans. It had not occurred to us to think any differently about Christmas, but she reminded us that this was a special time in our healing process and that we needed to rethink our previous rituals at the Trinity Foundation.

On Christmas Eve, Doug and I went to an Episcopal Church. At this time, we had only attended a few services and were still new to this type of worship. At the beginning of the service, the choir came in from the back of the church carrying candles that lit the darkened sanctuary and sang "Oh, Come, All Ye Faithful." As we rose to join in this traditional Christmas hymn, tears streamed down our faces and we reached for each other's hand. For the first time in years, we were both able to celebrate Christmas in its true meaning.

In the spring of 2001, we felt we had sufficiently worked through our issues and ended our sessions with Debbie.

Doug was working and attending graduate school and I was immersed in my career, which left little time to think about Trinity Foundation. Then, in the fall of that year, several events occurred which, once again, turned my life upside down. Within a little over two months both of my parents died and I lost my job after nineteen years in the public mental health system. I found myself back in counseling with Debbie. I also went to a grief/loss support group sponsored by the Visiting Nurses Association. Every week I would go to those groups, along with eight to ten other people who had also recently lost a loved one. We cried and we told our stories to each other. And at the end, I was at peace with the loss of my parents.

During one of my counseling sessions with Debbie, she told me that she felt that I had never completely grieved the loss of Trinity Foundation and suggested that I write a book about the experience. My sister, Joan, had suggested the same thing, but since I had never written a book, I thought the idea was preposterous. However, several weeks later, my friend Crystal was rushed to the hospital in critical condition. For the next four days, Crystal clung to life. One morning I woke up thinking about her and cried because I couldn't remember all the details of her experience with the Trinity Foundation and her struggle to leave the community. She had not regained consciousness after her admission to the hospital, and I realized I might never have the opportunity to talk with her again. I recalled the evening Doug and I had dinner with Crystal and her husband, Chad, several months after they left Trinity Foundation. Crystal related to us the events surrounding their exit. I remembered the sadness I felt and remarked to Doug that "we had failed them." "We" being the Trinity Foundation — Doug and I were still a part of Trinity at this time and I had a deep sense of remorse regarding how Crystal and Chad were treated and the lack of grace that Trinity showed them.

When Doug and I left Trinity just a couple of months after that dinner with Crystal and Chad, Crystal was my primary source of support. We talked a lot and e-mailed back and forth, which helped me process a lot of the emotions I was going through. Shortly after she died, I found an e-mail she wrote which gave me chill bumps. She wrote:

> I know there were many times I was there when you were shouted down or ridiculed into silence. That's why I asked if you'd written a letter to Ole as if you were sitting across from him and he couldn't interrupt you and his mannerisms meant nothing to you. Maybe the result would be the start of a great book. A book of enlightenment and not anger. It's those unsaid words, questions, and concerns that I believe your counselor wants you to get out. Not for Ole's sake, but for yours. And if it ends up for the benefit of someone else and God is using you (us) for that, then His will be done.
>
> Love always,
> Crystal

After finding this e-mail from Crystal, I knew I had to write a book. I did not know what shape or form the book would have—and only had a sense of urgency about writing about this unique time in our lives. My constant prayer was that it would be a "book of enlightenment and not anger"—which would be a means of helping others who have gone through a similar spiritually abusive experience.

In the midst of writing a book to help others, I stumbled into my grief recovery process. I began to go through the various stages of grief: denial, depression, bargaining, anger, and acceptance. Mental health professionals agree that the stages are not linear and an individual may go back and forth through the stages. Grief is a normal process in response to any loss, but grieving, in and of itself, does not necessarily lead to healing. The memoir Alice Sebold wrote of how her life drastically changed after being brutally raped during her college days, illustrates this. In her book, *Lucky*, Sebold talked about writing an article about her rape that was published in the *New York Times Magazine*. Many years later this piece was cited in Dr. Judith Lewis Herman's book, *Trauma and Recovery*, and when Sebold read Dr. Herman's book she noted that the book was divided into two parts: "Trauma" and "Recovery." Sebold's story was footnoted in the section on trauma, which jolted her into realizing that although she had done much of the work of grief, she had not yet crossed over into recovery. [5]

I interviewed former members and listened to the taped interviews over and over. Somehow, in listening to their stories, I began to feel all the emotions I had buried. I felt the sadness of losing a community who had been my family and friends. I felt the hurt of losing my vision of Christianity. I felt the anger of being betrayed. I felt the hurt and confusion of losing my way of life at Trinity Foundation. And I felt the pain that others who had left Trinity Foundation had experienced. Many days I longed to have a job or place I could go to each day where my memories where locked safely away, to a time when I didn't hear Ole's voice a thousand times a day. My emotions were all over the place and I grieved, but like Sebold, it was years before I crossed over into the recovery.

Psychoanalyst Erik Erikson, in his writings about the stages of life, suggested that the last major task in an individual's life is, "Integration versus Despair." He described this task as accepting the life that has been lived without regrets of the past. Erikson believed that without the successful completion of this task of integration, the individual was left with a sense of despair that his life was without meaning. [6] Although Erikson uses this concept specifically to describe life's final stages, it seems that this is a task we are called on to complete at various stages of our life. The task simply is to integrate the pieces of our past and accept the events that make up our life story. Failure to do this leads to despair.

When I finally realized I had to acknowledge the loss and embrace the whole experience, that it had to be worked through rather than worked around, I began the real journey back to God. My task today is to continue on this spiritual journey of hope and peace while struggling with all the doubts and fears. To recover my sense of who God is. To trust in His love. To sing, "Amazing Grace." To reclaim my birthright as His beloved. And to be able to hear His voice once again.

NOTES

Chapter 1

1. Michael Langone, editor. *Recovery from Cults: Help for Victims of Psychological and Spiritual Abuse* (New York: W. W. Norton & Company, 1993), 5.

2. Ibid.

3. Margaret Thaler Singer with Janja Lalich, *Cults in Our Midst* (San Francisco: Jossey-Bass Publishers, 1995), XIX.

4. Ibid., 17.

Chapter 4

1. Ibid., XX.

2. Len Oakes, *Prophetic Charisma: The Psychology of Revolutionary Religious Personalities* (New York: Syracuse University Press, 1997), 2–36.

3. Ibid., 45–50.

4. Ibid., 44–73.

5. Ibid., 44–73.

6. Casey Miller, "Terror of the Televangelists," *D Magazine*, April 1992.

7. Ibid.

8. Bill Hunter, "Chance Encounter Has Chain Reaction, *Dallas Morning News*, August 17, 1968.

9. Casey Miller, Terror of the Televangelists, *D Magazine*, April 1992.

10. N. T. Wright, *The New Testament and the People of God* (Minneapolis: Fortress Press, 1992), 16–17.

11. C. FitzSimons Allison, *The Cruelty of Heresy: An Affirmation of Christian Orthodoxy* (Harrisburg, PA: Morehouse Publishing, 1994), 11.

12. Joel Kramer, and Diana Alstad, *The Guru Papers: Masks of Authoritarian Power* (Berkeley, California: Frog, Ltd, 1993), 32–33.

13. Trevor Ravenscourt, *The Spear of Destiny* (York Beach, ME: Red Wheel/Weiser, 1973), 8–9.

14. Max Weber, *Economy and Society* edited by G. Roth and C. Wittich. 3 Vols. (New York: Bedminster Press, 1968a), 241–42.

Chapter 6

1. Robert Jay Lifton, *Thought Reform and the Psychology of Totalism: A Study of 'Brainwashing' in China* (Chapel Hill: University of North Carolina Press, 1989), 425–426.

Chapter 7

1. Jonathan Edwards, "Sinners in the Hands of an Angry God," 1741.

Chapter 8

1. C. FitzSimons Allison, *The Cruelty of Heresy: An Affirmation of Christian Orthodoxy* (Harrisburg, PA: Morehouse Publishing, 1994), 20–21.

Chapter 10

1. Stephen Arterburn and Jack Felton, *Toxic Faith: Understanding and Overcoming Religious Addiction* (Colorado Springs: Waterbrook Press, 1991, 2001), 19.

2. Ibid., 159.

Chapter 13

1. Paul Martin, "Post-Cult Recovery: Assessment and Rehabilitation," in *Recovery from Cults*, edited by Michael Langone (New York: W. W. Norton & Company, 1993), 208–209.

2. Madeline Tobias, "Guidelines for Ex-Members," in *Recovery from Cults*, edited by Michael Langone (New York: W. W. Norton & Company, 1993), 312.

3. Paul R. Martin, "Post-Cult Recovery: Assessment and Rehabilitation," in *Recovery from Cults*, edited by Michael Langone (New York: W. W. Norton & Company, 1993), 211.

Chapter 14

1. Madeleine Tobias and Janja Lalich, *Captive Hearts Captive Minds: Freedom and Recovery from Cults and Abusive Relationships* (Alameda, California: Hunter House, 1994), 48–54.

2. Robert Jay Lifton, *Thought Reform and the Psychology of Totalism: A Study of 'Brainwashing' in China* (Chapel Hill: University of North Carolina Press, 1989), 429–430.

3. Kathleen Norris, *Amazing Grace, a Vocabulary of Faith* (New York: Riverhead Books, 1998), 3, 65.

4. Paul R. Martin, "Dispelling the Myths: The Psychological Consequences of Cultic Involvement," *Christian Research Journal,* Winter/Spring 1989, 8.

5. Alice Sebold, *Lucky* (Boston, New York, London: Little, Brown & Company, 1999), 239.

6. Erik Erickson, *Childhood and Society* (New York and London: W. W. Norton & Company, 1950, 1963), 268–269.

BIBLIOGRAPHY

Allison, C. FitzSimons. *The Cruelty of Heresy: An Affirmation of Christian Orthodoxy.* Harrisburg, PA: Morehouse Publishing, 1994.

Arterburn, Stephen and Jack Felton. *Toxic Faith: Understanding and Overcoming Religious Addiction.* Colorado Springs: Waterbrook Press, 1991, 2001.

Chrnalogar, Mary Alice. *Twisted Scriptures: Breaking Free from Churches That Abuse.* Grand Rapids: Zondervan Publishing House, 1998, 2000.

Conway, Flo and Jim Siegelman. *Snapping: America's Epidemic of Sudden Personality Change.* New York: Stillpoint Press, 1995.

Edwards, Jonathan. "Sinners in the Hands of an Angry God." Sermon preached in Enfield, Massachusetts (later Connecticut), July 8, 1741.

Erikson, Erik. *Childhood and Society.* New York and London: W. W Norton, 1950, 1963.

Giambalvo, Carol. *Exit Counseling: A Family Intervention.* Bonita Springs, Florida: American Family Foundation, 1992.

Hassan, Steven. *Combatting Cult Mind Control.* Rochester, Vermont: Park Street Press, 1988.

Johnson, David and Jeff VanVonderen. *The Subtle Power of Spiritual Abuse.* Minneapolis: Bethany House Publishers, 1991.

Kramer, Joel and Diana Alstad. *The Guru Papers: Masks of Authoritarian Power*. Berkeley, California: Frog, Ltd, 1993.

Langone, Michael, editor. *Recovery from Cults: Help for Victims of Psychological and Spiritual Abuse*. New York: W. W. Norton & Company, 1993.

Lifton, Robert Jay. *Thought Reform and the Psychology of Totalism: A Study of 'Brainwashing' in China*. Chapel Hill: University of North Carolina Press, 1989.

Martin, Paul R. "Pitfalls to Recovery Post-Cult Recovery: Assessment and Rehabilitation." Langone, *Recovery from Cults*, 1993.

Martin, Paul R. "Dispelling the Myths: The Psychological Consequences of Cultic Involvement." *Christian Research Journal*. Winter/Spring 1989.

Miller, Casey. "The Terror of the Televangelists." *D Magazine*, April 1992.

Norris, Kathleen. *Amazing Grace, a Vocabulary of Faith*. New York: Riverhead Books, 1998.

Oakes, Len. *Prophetic Charisma: The Psychology of Revolutionary Religious Personalities*. New York: Syracuse University Press, 1997.

Ravenscourt, Trevor. *The Spear of Destiny*. York Beach, ME: Red Wheel/Weiser, 1973.

Singer, Margaret Thaler with Janja Lalich. *Cults in Our Midst*. San Francisco: Jossey-Bass Publishers, 1995.

Sebold, Alice. *Lucky*. Boston, New York, London: Little, Brown and Company, 1999.

Storr, Anthony. *Feet of Clay: A Study of Gurus*. New York: Free Press Paperbacks, 1996.

Tobias, Madeline. "Guidelines for Ex-Members." *Recovery from Cults*. Michael Langone, editor. New York: W. W. Norton & Company, 1993.

Tobias, Madeleine Landau and Janja Lalich. *Captive Hearts Captive Minds: Freedom and Recovery from Cults and Abusive Relationships*. Alameda, California: Hunter House, 1994.

Wright, N. T. *The New Testament and the People of God*. Minneapolis: Fortress Press, 1992.

Yancey, Phillip. *What's So Amazing about Grace?* Grand Rapids: Zondervan, 1997.

SUGGESTED READING

I. General Information Regarding Cults or Abusive Groups:

Bounded Choice: True Believers and Charismatic Cults, by Janja Lalich. Berkeley and Los Angeles: University of California Press, 2004.

Cults in Our Midst, by Margaret Thaler Singer with Janja Lalich. San Francisco: Jossey-Bass Publishers, 1995.

Churches That Abuse, by Ronald Enroth. Grand Rapids, Michigan: Zondervan, 1992.

Exposing Spiritual Abuse, Mike Fehlauer. Lake Mary, Florida: Charisma House, 2001.

The Subtle Power of Spiritual Abuse, by David Johnson and Jeff VanVonderen. Minneapolis, Minnesota: Bethany House Publishers, 1991.

Toxic Faith: Understanding and Overcoming Religious Addiction, by Stephen Arterburn and Jack Felton. Colorado Springs, Colorado: Waterbrook Press, 1991, 2001.

Twisted Scriptures: Breaking Free from Churches That Abuse, by Mary Alice Chrnalogar. Grand Rapids, Michigan: Zondervan Publishing House, 1998, 2000.

When God Becomes a Drug, by Father Leo Booth. New York: Jeremy P. Tarcher/Putnam, Penguin Putnam, Inc., 1991.

When Religion Becomes Evil, by Charles Kimball. San Francisco: HarperSanFrancisco, 2002.

II. Psychological Profiles of Cult Leaders:

Feet of Clay: A Study of Gurus, by Anthony Storr. New York: Free Press Paperbacks, 1996.

The Guru Papers: Masks of Authoritarian Power, by Joel Kramer and Diana Alstad. Berkeley, California: Frog, Ltd, 1993.

Prophetic Charisma: The Psychology of Revolutionary Religious Personalities, by Len Oakes. Syracuse, New York: Syracuse University Press, 1997.

III. Recovery Issues:

Captive Hearts Captive Minds: Freedom and Recovery from Cults and Abusive Relationships, by Madeleine Landau Tobias and Janja Lalich. Alameda, California: Hunter House, 1994.

Combatting Cult Mind Control, by Steven Hassan. Rochester, Vermont: Park Street Press, 1988.

Exit Counseling: A Family Intervention, by Carol Giambalvo. Bonita Springs, Florida: American Family Foundation, 1992.

Healing Spiritual Abuse: How to Break Free from Bad Church Experiences, Ken Blue. Downers Grove, Illinois: InterVarsity Press, 1993.

Recovery from Cults: Help for Victims of Psychological and Spiritual Abuse, edited by Michael Langone. New York: W. W. Norton & Company, 1993.

Releasing the Bonds: Empowering People to Think for Themselves, by Steven Hassan. Somerville, Massachusetts: Freedom of Mind Press, 2000.

Trauma and Recovery, by Judith Lewis Herman. New York: Basic Books, 1992.

IV. Brainwashing, Mind Control:

Battle for the Mind: A Physiology of Conversion and Brain-Washing, by William Sargant. Cambridge, Massachusetts: Malor Books, 1997.

The Psychology of Attitude Change and Social Influence, by Philip Zimbardo and Michael Lieppe. New York: McGraw-Hill, 1991.

Snapping: America's Epidemic of Sudden Personality Change, by Flo Conway and Jim Siegelman. New York: Stillpoint Press, 1995.

Thought Reform and the Psychology of Totalism: A Study of Brainwashing in China, by Robert Jay Lifton. Chapel Hill: University of North Carolina Press, 1989.

The True Believer, by Eric Hoffer. New York: Harper & Row, 1951.

V. Specific Cults

Aum Shinrik—Japan's Unholy Sect, by Rei Kimura. North Charleston, South Carolina: BookSurge Publishing, 2002.

Blinded by Deceit, by Joanne Hansen. Edina, Minnesota: Beaver's Pond Press, 2002.

Inside Out: A Memoir of Entering and Breaking Out of a Minneapolis Political Cult, by Alexandra Stein. St. Cloud, Minnesota: North Star Press of St. Cloud, Inc., 2002.

Heaven's Harlots: My Fifteen Years As a Sacred Prostitute on the Children of God Cult, by Miriam Williams. New York: William Morrow, 1998.

Mad Man in Waco: The Complete Story of the Davidian Cult, David Koresh and the Waco Massacre, by Brad Bailey and Bob Darden. Waco, Texas: WRS Publisher, 1993.

The Promise of Paradise, by Staya Bharti Franklin. Barrytown, New York: Station Hill Press, 1992.

Seductive Poison: A Jonestown Survivor's Story of Life and Death in the Peoples Temple, by Deborah Layton. New York: Anchor Books, 1998.

Soul Snatchers, by Jean-Mari Abgrall. New York: Algora Publishing, 1999.

RESOURCES

Apologetics Index Organization
Web: www.apologeticsindex.org

Cult Information Centre
BCM Cults
London WC1N 3XX
United Kingdom
Telephone: (081) 651-3322

Cult Information Services
Box 867
Teaneck, New Jersey 07666
Telephone: (201) 833-1212
Web: www.cultinformationservice.org

Freedom of Mind Resource Center
P.O. Box 45223
Somerville, Massachusetts 02145
Telephone: (617) 628-9918
Fax: (617) 628-8153
Web: www.freedomofmind.com

Info-Cult (Canada)
Resource Centre on Cultic Thinking
5655 avenue du Parc, Suite 208
Montreal, Quebec
Canada H2V 4H2
Telephone: (514) 274-2333
Web: www. infocult.org

International Cultic Studies Association (ICSA)
(Formerly AFF, American Family Foundation)
P.O. Box 2265
Bonita Springs, Florida 34133
Telephone: (239) 514-3081;
Fax: (732) 352-6818
Web: www.culticstudies.org

Probe Ministries
1900 Firman Drive, Suite 100
Richardson, Texas 75081
Telephone: (972) 480-0240; (800) 899-PROB
Web: www.probe.org

reFOCUS, Inc.
P.O. Box 2180, Flagler Beach, Florida 32136
Telephone: (386) 439-7541, Fax: (386) 439-7537
Web: www.refocus.org

Watchman Fellowship, Inc.
P.O. Box 13340
Arlington, Texas 76094
Telephone: (817) 277-0023; Fax: (817) 277-8098
Web: www.watchman.org

Wellspring Retreat & Resource Center
P.O. Box 67
Albany, Ohio 45710
Telephone: (740) 698-6277; Fax: (740) 698-2053
Web: www.wellspringretreat.org

Give the Gift of
I Can't Hear God Anymore
To Your Friends and Colleagues

☐ YES, I want _____ copies of *I Can't Hear God Anymore* for $14.95 each.

Include $4.00 shipping and handling for one book, and $1.95 for each additional book.

Residents of Texas must include applicable sales tax of 8.25%. Canadian orders must include payment in U.S. funds, with 7% GST added.

Payment must accompany orders. Allow one week for delivery.

My check or money order for
$ _____ **is enclosed.**

Please charge my

☐ Visa   ☐ MasterCard

Name _____

Address _____

City/State/Zip _____

Phone _____ E-mail _____

Card # _____ Expiration Date _____

Signature _____

Make your check payable and return to:
VM Life Resources
P.O. Box 126
Rowlett, TX 75030-126

For credit card orders, call 888-281-5170
or visit www.dallascult.com to place order